Dive
Into a Great Journey

Ready to share your story?

https://entrepreneurprime.co.uk
editor@entrepreneurprime.co.uk

entrepreneur prime
Empowers Globally

Builds global branding, reaching over 190 countries and thousands of platforms

A good book will keep you fascinated for days. A good bookshop for your whole life.

Waterstones

CONTENTS

Celebrating the Visionaries of Beauty

Exclusive Interviews and Expert Advice from Award-Winning Authors.

COVER STORY

The Power Of Simplicity In Skincare

Helen Morrison

Leads Frownies Into A New Era Of Innovation And Legacy

PUBLISHER: Beauty Prime, A Subsidiary of NewYox Media Group. North House, 257 Upper Street, N1 1FU London, United Kingdom t: +44 79 3847 8420 editor@beautyprime.co.uk II http://beautyprime.co.uk

EDITORIAL: Y. Brown, Editor-in-Chief, E. Wilson, Managing Editor, C. Rochelle, Art Editor, L. Green, Content Editor, Reporters: Heater Turner, Jack Wilson, Jenny Taylor , J. Evans, Amy Brown, Ben F. Oncu CONTRIBUTOS: Aden D., Claudine D. Reyes, Adrian T.

We assume no responsibility for unsolicited manuscripts or art materials provided from our contributors.

EDITOR'S LETTER

As we step into the new year of 2026, I'm delighted to welcome you to this inspiring issue of Beauty Prime, where we celebrate the visionary minds reshaping the beauty landscape with innovation, compassion, and a commitment to authenticity. In a world overflowing with trends and quick fixes, our focus this time is on the power of simplicity—proving that true transformation often lies in thoughtful, science-backed approaches that honour individuality and long-term wellbeing.

Our cover story spotlights **Helen Morrison**, the dynamic leader guiding Frownies into an exciting new chapter. Helen's dedication to blending legacy with cutting-edge innovation embodies the essence of timeless skincare, reminding us that less can indeed achieve more when it comes to nurturing our skin's natural vitality.

We're honoured to feature **Dr. Kaveri Karhade**, a trailblazer in dermatology who is revolutionising care for melanin-rich skin. Through her evidence-based philosophy, she dispels myths, prioritises affordability, and empowers patients with personalised treatments that build lasting confidence. Similarly, Jess Bowers captivates with her "less is more" ethos, drawing from global influences to craft non-invasive rituals that sculpt and soothe, proving that simplicity is the ultimate luxury

in skincare.

Dive into the world of aesthetic surgery with **Dr. Juris Bunkis**, whose decades of expertise at Orange County Plastic Surgery have set new standards in natural rejuvenation. His signature techniques and patient-centred innovations highlight the artistry behind transformative results. We also shine a light on **Amany and Engy**, the visionary sisters behind ANTY jewellery. Rooted in heritage and self-expression, their brand invites us to embrace pieces that tell personal stories, blending cultural narratives with modern elegance.

And don't miss the insights from **Masuma Z. Bukhari** and **Eunice Opoku,** whose journeys in beauty entrepreneurship and holistic care inspire us to think beyond the surface, fostering empowerment and inclusivity in every facet of self-care.

At Beauty Prime, we believe beauty is about more than appearance—it's a journey of self-discovery and empowerment. These stories remind us to approach our routines with intention, embracing diversity and sustainability along the way. Whether you're seeking expert advice on winter skincare or exploring bold new expressions of style, this issue is your guide to radiant living.

Thank you for being part of our community. Here's to a year of bold visions and beautiful transformations.

Y. Brown
Editor-In-Chif

Dr. Kaveri Karhade, reshaping dermatology for melanin-rich skin with expertise, empathy, and a passion for evidence-based care.

Photos courtesy of Dr. Karhade

Dr. Kaveri Karhade Shares Her Expertise On Transforming Melanin-Rich Skin Through Science-Backed Care

Changing The Face Of Dermatology With Science And Compassion

Dr. Kaveri Karhade revolutionises dermatology for melanin-rich skin, blending scientific innovation with patient-centred care while breaking misconceptions and promoting affordability, confidence, and long-term results in skin health.

By Ember Wilson

Dr. Kaveri Karhade is a true luminary in the field of modern dermatology, and it is with great pleasure that we spotlight her immense contributions in this issue of Beauty Prime. With a wealth of expertise honed through years of rigorous training and practice, Dr. Karhade has become a staunch advocate for science-driven, evidence-based care, rejecting fleeting trends in favour of approaches that deliver real, lasting results. Her work is uniquely impactful, particularly in addressing the often-underrepresented needs of melanin-rich skin—an area in which she has emerged as a trusted pioneer and advocate.

Beyond her clinical practice, Dr. Karhade's influence extends far and wide. From her role as a dermatology adviser to the esteemed Dr. Kathy Fields at Rodan + Fields to her groundbreaking research published in prominent journals, she has made it her mission to advance understanding and challenge outdated misconceptions. Her insights, often amplified through her social media channels, are a beacon of clarity and practicality in the complex world of skin health. Known for her thoughtful, patient-centred approach, she strikes a perfect balance between leveraging cutting-edge technology and emphasising affordability and minimal intervention—a philosophy that resonates deeply in today's

Continued *on page 10*

increasingly conscious beauty landscape.

In this conversation, Dr. Karhade shares her professional journey, dispels myths surrounding richly pigmented skin, and offers a glimpse into her methodical, science-based approach to dermatology. Her candid reflections and dedication to empowering others through education reinforce why she is one of the most respected voices in this field. Prepare to be inspired by her profound passion for reshaping the narrative of dermatologic care.

What inspired you to focus your dermatology practice on melanin-rich skin, and how has this shaped your approach to treating diverse skin types?

Melanin-rich skin has historically been somewhat excluded from the vast variety of treatment options, especially energy and laser-based treatments. Sadly, this has to do with education of dermatologists- as late as 2018, when I was finishing my training, I had very little exposure to and training with melanin-rich skin. Textbooks and articles have historically focused on lighter skin types. By now, most dermatologists are very well trained in managing lighter skin; however, there remains a continued lack of knowledge and comfort with managing the nuances of darker skin types. It has been very rewarding to be able to offer my melanin-rich patients treatments, and thus results, that other dermatologists have told them they couldn't do.

You emphasize affordability and minimizing procedures—how do you balance cutting-edge technologies like lasers and injectables with your goal of minimal, cost-effective interventions?

We are all trying to achieve and maintain as clear and as youthful skin as possible. I always look at the goal, which is maintaining that skin for even 20 years down the road. By considering a patient's particular circumstances, I like to recommend the fewest number of interventions necessary to work towards that goal. So I frequently discourage procedures that may give immediate improvement but no longer-term benefit. Ultimately it ends up being more affordable for the patient AND better for their skin in the long run- win-win!

In your experience, what are the most common misconceptions patients with richly pigmented skin have about cosmetic dermatology, and how do you address them?

People are afraid of side effects from devices such as lasers, and rightly so- richly pigmented skin IS at higher risk for hyperpigmentation, which is a particularly bothersome side effect in this patient population. They find comfort in knowing that by thinking

"Affordable, Effective, and Lasting – The Dermatology Secrets Behind Dr. Karhade's Success"

Transforming Skin, Changing Lives

– How Dr. Kaveri Karhade is Redefining Dermatology

kavimd.com

through the detailed science of the skin, it is indeed possible to mitigate that risk and still safely get results.

Could you walk us through a success story where a personalized treatment plan significantly transformed a patient's skin health or confidence?

There are honestly too many to count- this is something I experience every day, multiple times, and is the reason I do what I do. Skin shouldn't be about vanity- it's about confidence. It's surprisingly easier to reach than many realize. My favorite recurring story is of melanin-rich patients with acne scars on the face that I treat with a combination approach. Sometimes they don't have to tell me how happy they are, I see it in the bounce in their step at a follow up visit.

With your active role in both clinical practice and research, how do you integrate emerging dermatologic evidence into real-world treatments for conditions like acne scars or pigmentation?

The key is thinking about the science- always, all the time. We're never trying anything trendy or random- only very calculated risks are taken to slowly expand the boundaries of our knowledge, and only when the science of its likely safety and efficacy are strong.

How has your presence on social media impacted your practice, and what role do you see digital education playing in the future of dermatologic care?

Many of my patients follow me on social to learn from the tips and tricks I share, and myths that I like to bust. Digital education is very important in the future of dermatologic care; it is actually surprising that in 2025 there are still so many misconceptions out there about the basics of skin and skin care. We have a long way to go in educating the public.

Confidence Through Care

*Dr. Kaveri Karhade on the Power
of Personalised Treatments*

@dr_kavi_derm

"

Jess Bowers: The NYC-Based Aesthetician Redefining The Beauty Industry With Her Motto "Less Is More". Photo by Rhea Karam

Jess Bowers Redefines Skincare With Her "Less Is More" Philosophy

The Power Of Simplicity In Skincare

By Lyra Green

Jess Bowers shares her skincare philosophy, expertise in non-invasive treatments, and insights into global beauty cultures, offering simple yet effective solutions for achieving healthy, sculpted skin and ultimate wellbeing.

Jess Bowers needs little introduction to those familiar with the modern skincare world. A name synonymous with refined simplicity, Jess has redefined what it means to care for the skin with her legendary "less is more" philosophy. From her humble beginnings to becoming a sought-after aesthetician in both New York City and Paris, Jess epitomises expertise, precision, and a deeply intuitive understanding of skin health. Her gentle yet transformative techniques, combined with her passion for holistic wellbeing, have garnered her an international reputation amongst those fortunate enough to experience her artistry.

Having honed her skills at the prestigious Atelier Esthetique Institute of Esthetics in New York, Jess seamlessly blends science with the art of touch. Her remarkable ability to tailor her treatments to clients' individual needs speaks not only to her technical mastery but also to her dedication to achieving glowing, healthy skin without invasive measures. From gua sha to reiki, dermaplaning to customised sculpting, Jess approaches every face with a thoughtful and creative flourish that makes her work a true craft.

Whether she's demystifying common skincare misconceptions, simplifying routines for the jet set, or preparing to expand her practice to London, Jess Bowers continues to challenge conventional beauty standards while championing wellness and balance from the inside out. It is our privilege to highlight the brilliance of Jess in this issue of Beauty Prime Magazine. Her passion and vision inspire us to embrace simplicity, cultivate self-care, and redefine beauty as something much deeper than skin-deep.

You describe your philosophy as "less is more" when it comes to skincare. What inspired that approach and how has it shaped the treatments you offer?

Less is More, my motto and approach to skincare. It's how I've always approached skincare and have felt my best. Working with hundreds of clients I noticed the commonality of the more they put on the skin the more their skin barrier was disrupted causing irritations, redness and congestion backing up my theory of "Less is More".

Your bio mentions you were trained at the Atelier Esthetique Institute of Esthetics in New York City—how did that education inform your non-invasive and hands-on method?

Yes, I received my training and education at Atelier Esthetique Institute of Esthetics in New York City. My studies there focused heavily on the science of the skin, providing me with a strong foundation in skincare and esthetics. Building upon that education, I developed my own unique, non-invasive approach to treatment. This method is inspired by my personal experiences with various modalities of touch from around the world. I combined the most effective and soothing elements from each of these practices with my scientific understanding of the skin to create a deeply relaxing and highly effective non-invasive treatment experience.

Continued *on page 14*

Winter Skincare Tips

As the winter months roll in and the temperature drops, many of us notice a drastic change in our skin. Drier air, chilly winds, and artificial heat can strip away the skin's natural moisture, leaving it feeling dry, tight, and irritated. For women, maintaining a radiant and healthy complexion during winter requires a little extra care and attention. Below, you'll find practical skincare tips designed to combat winter's harsh effects and leave your skin soft, hydrated, and glowing.

1. Hydration is Key

One of the most critical steps in winter skincare is keeping your skin hydrated. Cold weather robs the skin of its natural oils, making it prone to dryness and even flaking. To keep your skin moisturized:

- **Choose a richer moisturizer:** Trade your lightweight summer lotion for a thick, hydrating cream or balm that locks in moisture throughout the day.

- **Incorporate hyaluronic acid:** This miracle ingredient draws water into your skin, offering an instant hydration boost. Apply it before your moisturizer for maximum effect.

- **Don't forget your body:** Use body creams or oils that provide deep restoration for dry areas like elbows, knees, and hands.

2. Sunscreen Isn't Just for Summer

It's a common misconception that sunscreen isn't necessary in winter. In reality, harmful UV rays can penetrate through clouds and be reflected by snow, increasing the risk of skin damage.

- Use a broad-spectrum sunscreen with at least SPF 30 on your face and exposed areas every day.

- Look for moisturizers with SPF to keep your skin both hydrated and protected.

3. Avoid Overly Hot Showers

There's nothing more comforting than a hot shower on a cold winter morning, but hot water strips the skin of natural oils, leaving it dry and irritated. Stick to lukewarm water when showering and always apply a moisturizer immediately after to lock in hydration.

4. Gentle Cleansing is Essential

During the winter months, the skin barrier becomes more delicate. Harsh cleansers can strip natural oils and exacerbate sensitivity and dryness. Switch to a mild, hydrating cleanser that won't disrupt your skin's natural pH balance. Cleansing once at night is often enough, as over-cleansing can contribute to dryness.

5- Exfoliate Wisely

Exfoliation helps remove dead skin cells that can pile up on the surface, leaving your skin dull and flaky. However, over-exfoliating can do more harm than good in winter.

- Stick to gentle exfoliation once or twice a week.

- Opt for chemical exfoliants (containing AHAs or BHAs) rather than physical scrubs, as they are less abrasive and better suited for dry or sensitive skin.

6. Layer Wisely with Serums

Just as you would layer your clothes in winter, consider layering your skincare products. Start with a hydrating serum rich in hyaluronic acid or ceramides to create the perfect base for your moisturizer. This technique ensures your skin stays hydrated and plump throughout the day.

7. Combat Winter Scalp Dryness

Don't forget the skin on your scalp! Winter air can leave it dry and itchy. Use a scalp treatment or add a nourishing hair oil to your routine to prevent flakiness and maintain a healthy scalp.

8. Drink Up!

No amount of external hydration can replace the importance of hydrating your body from within. Drink plenty of water and incorporate water-rich fruits like oranges and melons, which help keep your skin supple and glowing.

9. Invest in a Humidifier

Indoor heating systems can really dry out your skin. Using a humidifier can enhance the moisture levels in the air, creating a more skin-friendly environment, especially while you sleep.

10. Pamper Yourself with Masks

Add weekly hydrating masks to your routine to give your skin an extra moisture boost. Look for masks containing nourishing ingredients like honey, avocado, glycerin, or aloe vera for an added glow.

11. Protect Your Lips

Winter air can leave your lips cracked and sore. Always carry a hydrating lip balm with SPF in your bag to reapply throughout the day. For extra care, consider applying a thicker lip treatment at night to wake up to soft, smooth lips.

12. Don't Neglect Your Hands and Feet

Our hands and feet are often exposed to the elements, resulting in dry, cracked skin. Wear gloves and thick socks to protect these areas from the cold. Use a rich hand cream and a foot balm regularly, especially before bed.

13. Know Your Skin's Needs

Every woman's skin is unique, and a one-size-fits-all approach won't work for everyone. Pay attention to how your skin reacts to the colder weather and adjust your skincare routine accordingly. If you're unsure, consult a dermatologist for advice tailored to your specific skin type.

14. Be Kind to Your Skin

Finally, remember that self-care goes beyond skincare products. Getting enough sleep, reducing stress, and maintaining a balanced diet all play a significant role in the health and appearance of your skin.

This winter, don't let the elements steal your skin's glow. By taking a few extra steps and prioritizing hydration, you can enjoy a radiant, healthy complexion all season long. Whether braving the cold outdoors or cozying up indoors, your skin will thank you for the extra love and care.

Stay beautiful, stay glowing!

Jess Bowers: Aesthetician Extraordinaire Redefining Skincare With Her Elegant "Less Is More" Philosophy

You work in both NYC and Paris. How do the beauty cultures and client expectations differ between those cities, and how do you adapt your practice accordingly?

The main difference in the two cultures is in Europe they don't ask questions or for product recommendations. They receive treatment and go about their day. Whereas in the USA clients want to know how to better their skin quality and want product recommendations. More conversations in the USA vs Europe is the main difference

You've trained in gua sha technique, are a member of the Reiki Association, and are certified in dermaplaning and chemical peels—what role do these diverse modalities play in your philosophy of healthy, sculpted skin?

Yes I am trained in many modalities as all skin is different. If someone comes to me with a disrupted skin barrier or acne I need to address the skin first and foremost sometimes that needs a different approach. I think it's best to be trained and prepared for every client's needs.

What is one common skincare myth you encounter with clients, and how do you demystify it in your treatments or consultations?

That you need to wash your face multiple times throughout the day. I always tell clients if you wash your face in the evening before bed unless you are sleeping in dirt you should wake up with your skin at an almost perfect PH and there is no need to wash your face. However there are always expectations but for the most part spf is all you need in the morning.

For someone with a very busy lifestyle (traveling, city living, etc.), what are your top three skincare "musts" to maintain glow and resilience?

Sleep, Face Ice Baths in the morning and SPF. Simple and effective, it doesn't need to be complicated.

How do you decide which treatment is right for a client—what factors do you assess and what does the decision-making process look like?

I determine my approach by carefully observing and feeling the skin by its texture, tone, and areas of tension. It only takes a few moments to understand what each client's skin truly needs. Most people hold a surprising amount of tension in their face, so a sculpting and de-puffing treatment is often exactly what brings balance and vitality back to their complexion.

As someone redefining the beauty industry to help people "feel their best", how do you measure or observe the "feel-good" outcome beyond just visible results?

The "feel-good" result comes from guiding clients into a light, restorative trance through movement of massage on the face. When I sense that they've drifted into that peaceful state, somewhere between being awake and asleep I know they'll leave feeling their absolute best. I often say there are very few moments in life when we lie completely still on our backs, not quite asleep but fully at ease, and that stillness creates something profound. Think of it as the most transformative 60-minute meditation you can experience.

What emerging trend or technology in skincare excites you right now, and how do you integrate or evaluate new innovations for your clients?

Again I stick with my motto of less is more and at the moment I see a movement of clients moving away from the 12 step skincare routine. I see more digestibles in the skincare industry that excite me. Clients honing in on their internal health for an external glow.

Looking ahead, what are your goals for your practice—any new services, collaborations, or ways you want to evolve your work in the next few years?

I would love to expand to London, I've always been drawn to the city's unique energy and timeless elegance. I already have a wonderful client base there and it feels like the natural next step. I'm also developing a special product that I haven't shared publicly yet (ssshhh) something unique that isn't highlighted currently on the market. It's designed for everyone, regardless of gender or age, and I can't wait to bring it to life.

"Leading with purpose and passion, Helen Morrison, the fifth-generation President and CEO of Frownies, honours a legacy spanning 136 years while driving the brand into a new era of innovation and empowerment. With her family's commitment to natural, non-invasive skincare solutions at heart, and a personal mission to inspire confidence and authenticity, Helen's journey is a testament to the power of connection, community, and care.

Helen Morrison Leads Frownies Into A New Era Of Innovation And Legacy

The Power Of Simplicity In Skincare

By Lyra Green

Helen Morrison, President and CEO of Frownies, blends a rich family legacy, innovation, and authentic leadership to empower women while driving the brand's growth with non-invasive, effective skincare rooted in wellness.

Helen Morrison never fails to embody the perfect fusion of passion, purpose, and legacy. Sitting at the helm of Frownies as its newly appointed President and CEO, Helen brings not only a deep respect for the brand's 136-year heritage but also a modern vision that inspires growth and innovation. For over five generations, the women in Helen's family have poured their hearts into a company dedicated to providing effective, non-invasive skincare solutions, and Helen is now carrying that torch with pride, authenticity, and a clear commitment to empowering others.

Her years as a yoga instructor have given her a profound understanding of wellness, which she weaves seamlessly into Frownies' ethos. What stands out most about Helen, however, is her genuine warmth, her ability to create connection, and her passion for making a positive impact—not only within the beauty industry but also in the lives of those she touches. In this exclusive interview, we delve into Helen's journey, her vision for the future of Frownies, and the invaluable lessons she has carried forward from a legacy built on care, innovation, and trust. Prepare to be both inspired and uplifted by her incredible story.

Congratulations on your new role! How does it feel to step into the position of President and CEO as the fifth generation of your family to lead Frownies?

It's honestly so exciting but also very humbling and surreal. My grandmother and great-great-grandmother poured their hearts into this brand for over a century, and to carry that legacy forward is both an honor

and a responsibility I don't take lightly. For the past five years, I've lived and breathed this brand not just as a family member but as a content creator, brand ambassador, and the face of the brand, a true believer in what Frownies stands for.

Frownies is a brand with a remarkable 136-year legacy. How do you balance honouring the company's heritage while also focusing on modern innovation and growth?

For me, honoring heritage and driving innovation go hand in hand. Our legacy is all about innovation. My great-great-grandmother created Frownies in 1889, long before clean beauty was a trend and long before Botox or injectables were used for cosmetics. So today, when we're developing new products, updating packaging, or expanding channels, it's not about chasing trends, it's about translating her original philosophy into today's world, where women still want effective, non-invasive solutions that actually work.

What lessons have you learned from the previous generations of your family that you feel will guide you in this leadership role?

One of the biggest lessons that's been passed down to me is that taking care of people and building community is what matters most. Every generation before me has operated with personal connection at the center—writing handwritten letters, sending thank-you notes, taking customer calls dire-

Continued *on page 18*

"Innovation for us means using technology and sustainability in ways that feel human."
— Helen Morrison

ctly—and it's something we still do today. That authenticity has built a level of trust that's at the core of who we are. As I always say, people want to buy from someone they like, know, and trust. And when it comes to skincare and beauty, something so personal, our customers need that sense of connection and community.

How do you envision the future of Frownies under your leadership, and are there any specific goals you are particularly excited to achieve?

I would say that Frownies is already the most trusted name in non-invasive alternatives to injectables. But what excites me most is continuing to educate women on their options—to help younger women feel confident that they don't have to turn to cosmetic procedures like Botox and fillers at such a young age. I'm also always excited to deepen our relationship with customers and grow our community. I want every woman who discovers Frownies to feel like she's found a brand that truly understands her—one that celebrates aging with authenticity, honesty, a little humor, and a sense of empowerment instead of fear.

Frownies has recently gained viral attention. How has this impacted the brand, and how do you plan to engage with this growing audience?

At this point, we're about five years into viral attention—so it's really a community movement we've built online. As we've done from the start, we'll continue showing up with real, relatable content and genuine connection. Seeing people share their before-and-afters or their skepticism-turned-love for Frownies is priceless. We engage with that audience every day on social media as real people—not just a corporation or a business—and that will never change.

Helen's vision to empower younger women and champion alternatives to invasive cosmetic procedures.

"Beauty doesn't have to be complicated."
— Helen Morrison

Continued *on page 19* →

Frownies' legacy of non-invasive skincare innovation since 1889.

Continued *from page 18*

> *"People want to buy from someone they like, know, and trust."*
> *– Helen Morrison*

As the beauty market evolves, particularly with advances like AI and sustainability demands, how does Frownies plan to stay competitive and relevant?

Innovation for us means using technology and sustainability in ways that feel human. Whether it's exploring AI for better customer personalization or developing more eco-conscious packaging, the goal is always progress with purpose. Frownies has lasted 136 years because we've never been afraid to evolve, but we never lose sight of why we exist: to make effective, affordable, non-invasive skincare accessible to everyone.

What role do natural ingredients and wellness continue to play in Frownies' product offerings, and are there any new formulations or innovations on the horizon?

Natural ingredients and wellness are at the core of everything we do. Our products are designed to support the skin naturally. We have a few exciting innovations coming, including a full-face collagen mask. Our approach is always to keep the ingredient list intentional and natural, while also leaning into new, innovative ingredients that genuinely benefit the skin.

Can you share how Frownies' unique family ownership influences the company culture and customer relationships?

We're a team of real people who care deeply about the impact we make. That intimacy carries through to how we treat our customers—when someone messages us on Instagram, they're often chatting directly with someone from our actual team, not a bot or outsourced rep. We think of our customers as an extension of the Frownies family, and I believe that warmth and transparency are a big part of why our community feels so loyal.

Skincare is a highly saturated industry. What would you say sets Frownies apart from other brands in the market?

What sets Frownies apart is our history, our community, and our results. In a market flooded with influencers promoting the next big fad, we lead with generations of real women getting real results. We focus heavily on building relationships with our customers and truly connecting with them—something people might say isn't scalable. But as we've 10X'd the brand, we've proven that connection is scalable when it's genuine, because it's at the heart of everything we do.

If your great-great-grandmother, Margaret Krosen, could see what Frownies has become today, what do you think she would say?

I think my great-great-grandmother would probably be in shock seeing what her dream has become. Who starts a brand and imagines that 130 years later it would still be run by their great-great-granddaughter? It's pretty remarkable. But more than anything, I think she'd be proud—that we've stayed true to her mission of providing women with tools to care for themselves naturally, helping them feel confident and beautiful in their own skin. She built Frownies on the belief that beauty doesn't have to be complicated, and I like to think she'd say, "You've kept my dream alive—and made it even bigger."

Celebrating Decades Of Expertise In Aesthetic Surgery

DR. JURIS BUNKIS

Showcases Innovation And Excellence At Orange County Plastic Surgery

By Ember Wilson

Dr. Bunkis' path from Harvard-trained surgeon to a globally recognised innovator in plastic surgery.

The philosophy behind his signature "A to V" Facelift for natural results in facial rejuvenation.

His dedication to advancements in patient-centred care, including cutting-edge technologies and surgical techniques.

Contributions to medical research with 40+ publications and numerous textbook chapters.

Dr. Juris Bunkis stands as an inspiring figure in the field of aesthetic medicine, with a career that spans decades of surgical expertise, academic distinction, and compassionate patient care. A pioneer in the realm of plastic surgery, Dr. Bunkis has never been content with simply maintaining the status quo. Instead, he has driven forward innovation, combining artistry with science to revolutionise the landscape of facial rejuvenation and achieve transformative, natural-looking results for his patients.

An alumnus of prestigious institutions such as the University of Toronto and Harvard University, Dr. Bunkis has cultivated a legacy of excellence that transcends borders. His renowned "A to V" Facelift represents the kind

Dr. Juris Bunkis shares his journey of innovation in aesthetic surgery, the philosophy of natural beauty, and the future vision for Orange County Plastic Surgery's growth and patient care.

of originality and dedication that defines his career, blending knowledge, precision, and a deep understanding of human anatomy to restore harmony and confidence in his patients. With over 40 scientific publications and contributions to numerous medical textbooks, his thought leadership reverberates throughout the global medical community, while his voluntary roles as a deputy sheriff and Honorary Consul for Latvia reflect a profound commitment to service beyond his profession.

It is our privilege at *Beauty Prime* to showcase the journey and vision of a surgeon who has not only mastered his craft but also shaped the transformative potential of plastic surgery. Dr. Bunkis exemplifies the perfect balance of innovation, compassion, and expertise, making him an unparalleled leader in the field and an inspiration to practitioners and patients alike.

What inspired you, Dr. Bunkis, to establish Orange County Plastic Surgery, and how has the practice evolved since its founding?

I taught at the University of California, San Francisco after completing my training at Harvard University. In 1983, I went into an aesthetic private practice in the San Francisco Bay Area. This practice grew tenfold and I was very happy there. But in the year 2000, my son, who was a very good baseball player, was scouted by a few college coaches, who suggested he attend high school in southern California. I did not want to send him off to high school by himself, so we sold our Bay Area practice, decided to move to Orange County and I started Orange County Plastic Surgery. Within two years, Orange County Plastic Surgery was exceeding the revenue I was producing in Northern California, and OCPS has done nothing but grow since.

Dr. Ekstrom, after 30 years practicing in New England, what drew you to join Orange County Plastic Surgery, and how has your experience here compared to your previous work?

I was drawn to California after practicing in New England for more than 35 years by my partner in work and life. I now practice with him here in California and we each energize the other when it comes to the practice of plastic surgery. We enjoy bouncing opinions and experiences off each other and being in the operating room together, trading information on techniques and outcomes. It is very energizing for both of us!

While there are some differences between the two geographies....for example New England is more conservative in the approach to appearance, and Californians take enhancement of appearance as a given....at

Continued *on page 22*

Dr. Juris Bunkis, renowned plastic surgeon, partners with
Dr. Deborah Ekstrom, founder of Money Loves Women
and President of Salisbury Plastic Surgery, combining expertise
to empower beauty, confidence, and transformation.

Continued *from page 20*

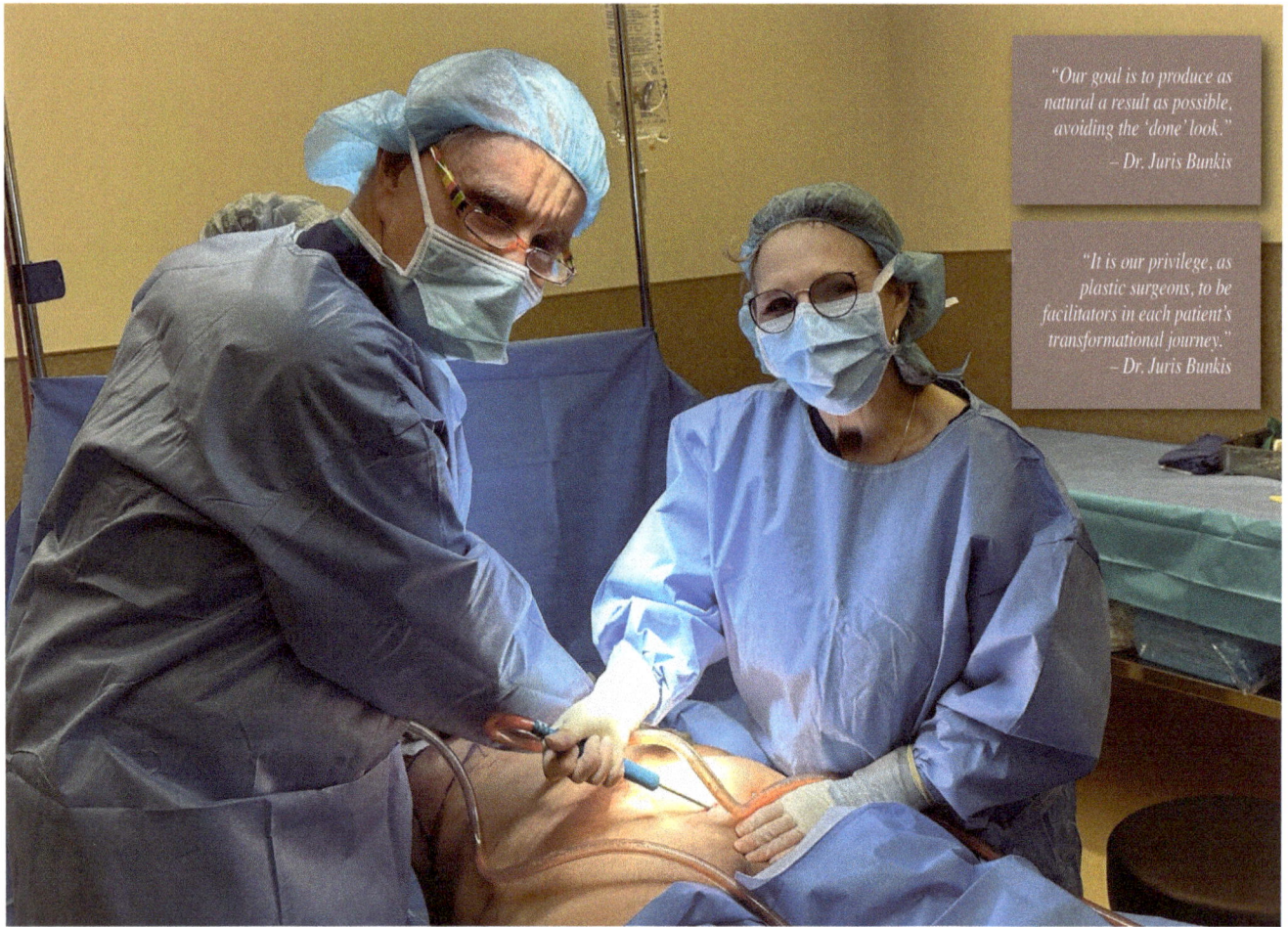

"Our goal is to produce as natural a result as possible, avoiding the 'done' look."
– Dr. Juris Bunkis

"It is our privilege, as plastic surgeons, to be facilitators in each patient's transformational journey."
– Dr. Juris Bunkis

Photo: Dr. Juris Bunkis, global leader in aesthetic surgery, transforming faces and lives with artistry, precision, and compassionate care.

both locations most people are just focused on presenting themselves at their best and being comfortable in their skin in order to maximize their confidence. Higher confidence, of course, is associated with increase success in all areas of life. It is our privilege, as plastic surgeons, no matter where we are, to be facilitators in this transformational journey, and it is both humbling and rewarding, regardless of locale.

With such a wide range of procedures offered at Orange County Plastic Surgery, how do you both decide which new techniques and technologies to adopt?

We both do the entire gamut of aesthetic procedures, frequently do larger procedures together ("team surgery") which is a major advantage to patients as it lessen OR time and cost. But we do have areas of interest that differ. Dr. Bunkis prefers procedures above the clavicles - facial rejuvenation, rhinoplasties, otoplasties, blepharoplasties, brow lifts, etc. Dr. Ekstrom specializes in body contouring, breast surgery, surgery to correct deformities from massive weight loss, microfat grafting, and the various radiofrequency and J-Plasma procedures. We both evaluate new technologies before adopting

them, both try new techniques and evaluate them (keep what is better that what we used to do, abandon methods that do not provide an advantage to our patients.

Dr. Bunkis, your Natural A to V Facelift is unique to your practice—can you share the story behind its development and what sets it apart?

A youthful face is V shaped, with fullness in the cheeks, tapering down towards the jaw line. As we age, the underlying muscles sag and pull overlying skin and fat with the muscles as they descend, leading to a more A shaped face, with fullness over the jowls and neck laxity. Our A to V Facelift, sometimes utilizing supplemental microfat grafting, is designed to reposition the sagging muscles and fat back up into the cheek area, restoring a youthful V shaped face. Our goal is to produce as natural a result as possible, avoiding the "done" look.

Dr. Ekstrom, your work in "quick recovery" breast augmentation and in-office liposuction is notable—what motivated you to focus on these patient-centered innovations?

My focus on "quick recovery" breast

augmentation centers around the increasing desires of women to undergo their procedures and get back to their lives.... professional, fitness, and family activities as smoothly and quickly as possible in order to pursue their personal success goals. In addition, I am always looking for ways to make every patient's recovery as pain and stress free as possible. The quick recovery breast augmentation fills the bill!

Looking ahead, what are your shared goals for Orange County Plastic Surgery's future growth, both in terms of patient care and broader contributions to the field of plastic surgery?

We continue to teach students regularly and have plastic surgeons from around the globe visit our practice on a regular basis. Our goal is to provide a concierge experience for our patients and to treat each patient, as we ourselves would expect to be treated. Surgical excellence is a given. We are both in our 70's and know that our surgical careers will be over in the next five years or so, but as long as we continue to work, we expect to continue providing each of our patients a platinum experience and to give them better results than they could get elsewhere!

The Art of Storytelling

Emma Sadler Transforms Her Passion For Pets And Art Into A Meaningful Business

Emma Sadler, founder of Taleology, shares her journey of creating bespoke pet portraits, overcoming challenges, and fostering community through art and storytelling.

BY EDITOR'S DESK | LONDON

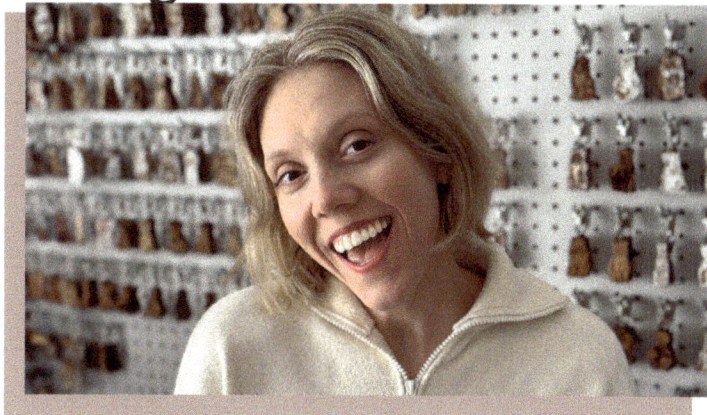

Emma Sadler, the visionary founder of Taleology, is an inspiring entrepreneur whose journey is marked by creativity, resilience, and a deep passion for storytelling. After facing setbacks in her career as a UX/UI designer, Emma took a bold leap into the world of bespoke pet portraits and storytelling, leading to the birth of Taleology. This venture was not only a professional pivot but also a heartfelt tribute to her late father's artistic legacy.

A Leap of Faith

Emma's inspiration to start Taleology stemmed from a combination of personal experiences and a desire to create something meaningful. After being laid off for the second time in two years from her UX/UI design job, she realized it was time to pour her heart and soul into a business that had already seen a successful test run. The idea of creating tangible pet portraits, particularly one of her dog Tommy, without the use of color, was a driving force behind her vision. Emma recalled her childhood memories of searching for her name in souvenir shops and wanted to build an inclusive experience for all pet owners, one that extended beyond the confines of the internet.

Moreover, Emma's late father, an incredible fine artist who never pursued his passion due to self-doubt, played a significant role in her motivation. By taking a chance on herself and her artistry, Emma feels she is honoring her father's potential and legacy.

Overcoming Challenges

Launching Taleology was not without its challenges. Emma faced the daunting unknowns of creating a product that was not consumable but rather an artistic expression. The subjective nature of art left her uncertain about whether anyone would appreciate her work. However, the success of her first pop-up event proved her wrong and fueled her determination to continue exploring new mediums.

Another ongoing challenge is navigating the social media landscape. Emma acknowledges the necessity of being present on social platforms for advertising and community building, and she is continually learning how to effectively engage with her audience online.

Commitment to Quality and Authenticity

At the heart of Taleology is a commitment to quality and authenticity. Emma ensures that all products are either produced in-house or sourced from small businesses, reinforcing her mission to support fellow artists and entrepreneurs. She is dedicated to using natural materials, consciously avoiding plastic to minimize environmental impact. This commitment to sustainability is a core principle of Taleology, guiding the development of new products and ensuring they align with her values.

A Unique Experience

What sets Taleology apart from other storytelling or narrative-driven brands is its bespoke nature. Emma emphasizes that no two items are truly the same, even if they feature similar artwork.

> *Emma Sadler is a visionary entrepreneur whose creativity and dedication to authenticity inspire others to pursue their passions and make a positive impact.*

The use of natural materials adds a unique touch to each piece, making every portrait a one-of-a-kind creation. Additionally, Taleology advocates for pet influencers to source locally, providing them with unique offerings for their communities while fostering a sense of connection and storytelling.

Looking Ahead

As Emma envisions the future of Taleology, she is excited about the prospect of a pop-up storefront experience in New York City. With plans to create a safe space for pet parents and engage with the community, this expansion represents a significant milestone for the brand. Currently, Emma is preparing for holiday markets, focusing on pop-up events throughout NYC, particularly in Brooklyn.

Engaging with the Community

Customer feedback plays a crucial role in the evolution of Taleology's offerings. Emma actively engages with her audience through Instagram stories to gauge interest in new products, often presenting multiple variations. While not every launch may succeed, she values the importance of community engagement and demonstrates a willingness to adapt based on customer input. Feedback collected during pop-up events also informs design changes, ensuring that Taleology remains responsive to its audience's needs.

Emma Sadler's journey with Taleology is a testament to the power of creativity, community, and the unique bond between pets and their owners. Through her artistry and commitment to authenticity, Emma continues to craft meaningful experiences that celebrate the individuality of beloved pets. As Taleology evolves, it stands as a beacon of innovation and determination, inspiring others to embrace their passions and create a positive impact in the world.

Emma Sadler, founder of Taleology, passionately creating bespoke pet portraits that celebrate the unique bond between pets and their owners.

Beauty rituals offer more than just surface transformation—they promote mental clarity, emotional grounding, and self-expression, helping to reduce stress and enhance confidence for a healthier, happier mind.

Beauty & Mental Health

How Simple Rituals Can Boost Mood, Calm Anxiety, and Reclaim Confidence

By Lyra Green

Why Beauty Routines Matter for Mental Health

In media and on feeds, beauty is often framed as skin-deep — a list of fixes to make you look a certain way. But the act of caring for yourself has a quieter, more powerful effect: beauty rituals can be meaningful tools for mental wellbeing. Whether it's a five-minute ski care routine, a signature scent, or the chance to play with makeup, small beauty practices can calm the mind, anchor the day, and help repair a frazzled sense of self.

• **Predictability and control:** Daily rituals create structure. When life feels chaotic, a simple morning or evening routine offers something reliable and accomplishable, which decreases stress and restores a sense of agency.

• **Sensory grounding:** Touch, scent, and slow breathing during a facial massage or shower engage the body's sensory system and help bring attention back to the present — a built-in form of mindfulness.

• **Neurochemical benefits:** Pleasant sensory experiences trigger the release of feel-good neurotransmitters (like dopamine and oxytocin) and can lower stress hormones for a short-term mood lift.

• **Self-expression and identity:** Makeup, hair styling, or choosing outfits are ways to explore identity and creativity. Looking like who you feel like being can reinforce confidence and social belonging.

• **Ritual as self-respect:** Consistently caring for yourself sends a message — to yourself — that you matter. That small act of compassion is cumulative.

Continued *on page 26*

Continued *from page 25*

"When we look good to ourselves, we often begin to feel good within."

Photo Credit: Courtesy Of Frownies

What the Research and Experts Say

Psychologists and wellbeing researchers increasingly recognize the therapeutic value of routine and ritual. Studies show that predictable, meaningful rituals — even modest ones — reduce anxiety and help people cope with uncertainty. Therapeutic approaches, including behavioral activation in depression treatments, often incorporate small, pleasurable activities (like grooming) because they reliably improve mood. While beauty practices are not a substitute for clinical care, they can complement therapy, medication, or other supports.

Continued *on page 27*

"Self-care is not selfish; it's an act of self-respect and resilience."

What the Research and Experts Say

- **Five-minute mindfulness skincare:** Turn cleansing and moisturizing into a sensory exercise. Focus on texture, temperature, and scent. Breathe slowly and notice how your skin responds. Even short, attentive routines lower reactivity and cultivate calm.

- **Scents for mood:** Fragrance can be a quick mood elevator. Citrus often feels energizing, lavender is calming, and vetiver or sandalwood can ground.

- **Massage and touch:** Scalp massage during shampooing, facial massage with a gua sha or your fingers, or hand care with a rich cream all activate touch receptors linked to relaxation.

- **Five-minute mindfulness skincare:** Turn cleansing and moisturizing into a sensory exercise. Focus on texture, temperature, and scent. Breathe slowly and notice how your skin responds. Even short, attentive routines lower reactivity and cultivate calm.

- **Scents for mood:** Fragrance can be a quick mood elevator. Citrus often feels energizing, lavender is calming, and vetiver or sandalwood can ground.

- **Massage and touch:** Scalp massage during shampooing, facial massage with a gua sha or your fingers, or hand care with a rich cream all activate touch receptors linked to relaxation.

- **Makeup as play:** When done with permission from yourself, makeup can be creative and empowering. Try a color you've never worn, or simplify to a "signature" look.

- **Haircare as signal:** A haircut, a simple styling ritual, or even brushing through tangles mindfully can mark transitions.

- **Digital boundaries:** Pair beauty rituals with tech limits. A no-phone 20 minutes before bed combined with a calming routine improves sleep — and skin.

- **Sleep-first beauty:** Prioritizing sleep is the single most effective "beauty" practice.

Photo Credit: Courtesy Of Frownies

Continued *on page 28*

Continued *from page 27*

Navigating the Downsides

Beauty can also stress the mind when linked to relentless comparison or perfectionism. If your routine becomes another metric for self-worth, pause. Healthy beauty practice is sustainable, affordable, and flexible.

Colourful Makeup Looks: Playful & Vibrant Styles

Photo by Mikhail Nilov

Continued *on page*

> "Simple practices like mindful skincare can do wonders for your mental health."

Photo by Mikhail Nilov

How to Build a Nourishing Routine

- Start small: Pick one 2–10 minute ritual and do it daily for two weeks.
- Make it meaningful: Attach your ritual to a cue.
- Prioritize pleasure over perfection.
- Budget for what matters.
- Share when helpful.

A Simple 7-Day Beauty + Wellbeing Challenge

Day 1: Five-minute mindful cleanse every night.

Day 2: Choose a signature scent and wear it intentionally.

Day 3: Try a two-minute scalp or face massage.

Day 4: Do one bold or playful makeup stroke — experiment.

Day 5: No screens 60 minutes before bed + calming skincare.

Day 6: Wear something that makes you feel confident.

Day 7: Reflect in a short journal entry about how these moments felt.

Beauty and mental health overlap in the quiet moments of care. Rituals don't erase hard days, but they do create islands of calm, touch, and self-respect that accumulate into resilience. Start small, be gentle with yourself, and let your beauty routine be a practice in tending to the person who deserves care most: you.

If low mood or anxiety persists, seek professional help.

Perry Offer shares his journey of resilience and his visionary approach to simplifying business processes, revolutionising companies, and promoting focused strategies to thrive in an increasingly complex global marketplace.

Perry Offer Simplifies Success With His Revolutionary Approach to Business

"Keep focused on your original concept. Don't let the chaos of the world force you to lose sight of your goals."

In today's fast-paced and often over-complicated business world, few individuals possess the rare ability to cut through the chaos and redefine success with clarity and precision. Perry Offer, a trailblazing entrepreneur and visionary leader, has mastered the art of simplifying complex processes to drive lasting results. With a career shaped by resilience and innovation, Perry's insights into problem-solving, leadership, and strategy have transformed struggling businesses into thriving industry leaders. In this exclusive interview, *Entrepreneur Prime* explores the principles that underpin Perry's remarkable journey, offering valuable lessons for entrepreneurs and business leaders navigating the challenges of a rapidly evolving global market.

You've emphasized the importance of simplicity in business and life. Can you share some examples from your career where simplicity led to success?

I have never been a half-hearted person. If I take something on I just have to give it my best shot, take a real interest in whatever I am working on and consider ways to make the process more streamlined and the company's revenue stronger and more efficiently earned. I have always been quite revolutionary and I still am. I had a book-keeping client called Wood Hosiery with whom I was then offered a full-time job as Director of Finance. That was in 1981 and I was only 22 but was ahead of my years in understanding the needs of such a role and, more importantly, the needs of the company.

One of the very good things about this company was that they recognised the need to evolve.

As an example, the company was doing well but stagnating a little. Stagnation means that things start to go backwards, profit margins begin to narrow and the roadway to problems beckons. So, the situation needed a review and with my prompting we discovered a way in which we could improve profits and service at the same time without jeopardising what we already had.

We found that our most profitable area was supplying to retailers on what was basically an own-label basis. I did quite a lot of research into the problems that retailers had with this and looked into ways in which we could offer a better system.

One of the major problems was that taking orders for 100 boxes of light tan tights and 100

Perry Offer's relentless drive, innovative solutions, and commitment to simplicity have solidified him as a transformative force in business.

---

boxes of dark tan tights meant that the tights were being made individually to colour and this taking several weeks to deliver. My research showed that if we simply had a large quantity of white tights in one place and could just dye them to order it meant that we could deliver in a few days rather than a few weeks. It made a massive difference to the extent that we were supplying a million pairs a week. We had become specialists in this market and were looked upon, quite rightly, as THE supplier to go to.

At just six years old, you felt the need to take responsibility for your family. How did that early experience influence your approach to leadership and problem-solving?

To be honest, at six years old my first thought was that I now had to take care of myself. I didn't think of the family at this point but hopefully, they did indeed benefit from my efforts. I mostly felt the need to be independent, as confident as I could be and especially to recognise that changes were needed and that I needed to be willing to embrace them.

I think that was a very good lesson for me and I try to pass this while approach on to others. Did I want my father to walk out? Of course not. In business there are many things which nobody actually wants to happen but they do and burying one's head in a bunker on the golf course achieves nothing but increasing the problem. Face

it, prepare to change and get on with it. Of course, if you see it coming, that's even better.

You've described British business as being in decline due to over-complication and mismanagement. What concrete steps can businesses or governments take to reverse this trend?"

In a word – simplify! Easier said than done? No, not at all. Step back from your business and survey it and you will soon see the knots of complication that breed inefficiency. Iron them out. At the same time, express yourself to others who can make changes. For instance, we all have MPs and government offices around us. Urge the Government to stay out of free markets. Also, on going regulation and changes of policy are among the biggest sources of unwanted and unessential complications. The lack of simplicity and the uncertainty it spawns is one of the biggest single sources of diminishing confidence which itself stymies investment plans and job creation.

Ask yourself, is it more complicated to run a business – any business – now than it was ten years ago. Every step of the way new methods, new legislation has been introduced to allegedly simplify things. The reality is that it has caused the roadway to failure to become a motorway.

In your opinion, how can companies strike the right balance between embracing modern technologies like AI and maintaining simplicity?

That is a key point. Let us consider AI in particular. What is it? It is a tool – that's it. Think of it as a tool and it will remain uncomplicated. Start to think of it as a member of the staff and you will start to complicate matters. It is the same for any form of technology. Use it but keep it in its place.

If your strategy is to simplify your business in the first place then you will already recognise AI and similar technology is simply a tool. Don't let it become more important than that or it will soon want your job – or your business!

Having worked with businesses of all sizes globally, what are the most common mistakes companies make when they find themselves in crisis?

The most common mistake is opting for incremental changes to the already over-complicated business. The lack of simplicity has already likely created the crisis. It is like a form of pollution. Why add more pollution? If businesses address the more fundamental changes involved in simplification that would lead them out of the crisis. Of course, businesses and their problems are variable but the principles of recovery are near enough all the same.

You argue that political correctness and red tape are strangling British businesses. Can you explain how these factors are affecting business performance and innovation?

Yes, as I have said before, simplicity is the only way forward. Who is going to win the marathon? Will it be the runner who is dressed for the part or will it be the runner who is wearing an overcoat and carrying a suitcase full of things he doesn't need? I know that is a very basic explanation but many businesses are carrying baggage that is neither wanted nor needed. Some of it has become legally obligatory – more and more lengthy forms to fill in. Some of it has been 'sold' as vital or your business will fall behind. Really? How have you survived this long? You started with simplicity and you succeeded. Now you are struggling because you lost touch with your original thinking. The result is that you spend so much time biting your nails that you are no longer innovative.

Your philosophy advocates for cutting through chaos and focusing on essentials. If you were guiding a start-up today, what are the three core principles you'd advise them to adopt?"

There are three main points.

A. Pick just one business niche where if you get 5% of demand it will mean that you will actually over-achieve on your exit target.

B. Identify the one dimension of product or service delivery that is most important to the most valuable potential customers in that niche.

C. Deliver consistently on that dimension and sell when you hit your target valuation. When you have reached the top of Everest you stop climbing, remove yourself and find another challenge to climb. I guess the message is, "Well done but don't be greedy."

Looking at the current state of global commerce, what do you see as the biggest opportunities and threats for businesses in the coming decade?

One of the biggest challenges is having the nerve to remain focussed in an increasingly fast-moving world. Opportunities might seem to appear like snow flakes but try to pick one up! Often people give up because their idea does not seem to be working. Analyse, is the idea still a good one? If so then it is the methodology that needs changing, probably simplifying. The whole world is in the grip of complication but you don't have to subscribe to it. Keep focussed on your original concept.

The biggest threat is the bankruptcy of governments along with the increasingly unstable political and geopolitical landscape.

With so much nonsense going on, there has never been a more important time or need for simplicity.

Source: Entrepreneur Prime

"

"Amany, the visionary co-founder of ANTY, blending heritage and modernity to create timeless designs that celebrate individuality."

Photos courtesy of Anty

Amany And Engy Of ANTY Transform Jewellery Into Stories Of Identity And Empowerment

Sisters Leading The Way In Luxury Design

Amany and Engy, founders of ANTY, blend heritage, individuality, and empowerment to create bespoke fine jewellery that tells personal stories and connects deeply with wearers across the globe.

By Ember Wilson

Amany and Engy Afify are visionaries who have not just built a jewellery brand, but a movement that celebrates individuality, heritage, and empowerment. As the founders of ANTY, these two remarkable women have redefined what it means to wear jewellery—not as a mere accessory but as a personal statement of identity and self-expression. They have challenged conventions and placed the wearer at the heart of every design, breathing life into pieces that tell unique stories. ANTY isn't just jewellery; it's a connection to culture, craftsmanship, and creativity.

What makes their journey even more inspiring is the boldness with which Amany and Engy have carved their paths in an industry traditionally dominated by men and legacy players. Their shared ability to merge personal experiences and global influences into distinctive designs is a testament to their ingenuity and rich backgrounds. From Amany's grounding in international development and her deep understanding of eastern and western aesthetics to Engy's dynamic allure as a model and her fearless transition into fine jewellery, both women bring an extraordinary duality to their craft. Together, they are shaping not just a brand but a legacy that resonates with beauty, resilience, and purpose.

In the interview to follow, we delve deeper into the heart of ANTY, exploring the moments that led to its creation, the values that guide it, and the powerful impact it has had on customers and collaborators alike. Prepare to be captivated by Amany and Engy's story—a story about passion, artistry, and the transformative power of

seeing and celebrating "you." It is our honour to share this journey with you in this edition of Beauty Prime.

Amany and Engy are trailblazers in the jewellery industry, crafting meaningful, culture-inspired designs that celebrate individuality and women's empowerment.

ANTY was born from your personal journey as an immigrant and your passion for design. Can you share a specific moment or turning point when you realized this dream had to become a business?

As an immigrant arriving in the U.S. at 27, I came with a strong sense of style shaped by my Egyptian roots and global travels. I always had a distinct taste in jewelry and

Continued *on page 34*

Continued *from page 33*

fashion, often designing my own pieces. While my government career kept me busy, the pandemic created a pause—just as I had moved to the U.S. and left my job. That moment gave me the space to reflect and finally ask: what if I turned my lifelong passion into something real? That's when ANTY was born—a brand rooted in identity, heritage, and self-expression.

You chose "ANTY" to center the brand around the idea of "YOU." How do you translate that concept into the customer experience, from design consultations to packaging?

Even if two people wear the same piece, it tells a different story on each of them. Style reflects who we are—our taste and how we want to be seen. That's why we chose "ANTY," which means "you" in Arabic. We produce most pieces in limited quantities and offer custom design services where we listen, iterate, and bring each client's vision to life. Every bespoke order is supported by a dedicated client ambassador. Even our packaging is part of the experience—thoughtfully designed to feel personal, elegant, and made just for you.

ANTY's identity is strongly tied to heritage, empowerment, and storytelling. How do you ensure these themes stay central as the brand grows and expands into new markets like Dubai?

At ANTY, our roots are our compass. Every collection is born from a personal or cultural narrative, with heritage and empowerment woven into the design. As we grow into new markets like Dubai, we remain intentional—partnering with retailers who value storytelling and aligning with customers who seek meaning in their jewelry. Whether through bespoke experiences, curated launches, or culturally resonant campaigns, we ensure our voice stays authentic and connected to the values that shaped us.

What has been the most rewarding or surprising response you've received from a customer about how ANTY jewelry made them feel seen or represented?

One of the most rewarding moments came when a client looked at a necklace and simply said, "Wow, it's so different." What stood out was not just the compliment—it was how deeply personal her reaction was. She said the piece made her feel incredibly special, like it truly suited her style in a way most jewelry never had. It wasn't just about aesthetics—it was about identity. She felt recognized, like the design spoke to a part of her that's often

"Engy Afify, the fearless co-founder of ANTY, bringing bold creativity and a passion for self-expression to every design."

Continued *on page 35*

"Blending heritage and empowerment into every piece
—meet ANTY."

Continued *from page 34*

overlooked in mainstream fashion. That moment reminded me why ANTY exists: to create jewelry that isn't just worn, but that makes people feel understood, represented, and uniquely seen.

As sisters and co-founders, how do you balance creative disagreements or business decisions while maintaining a strong family dynamic?

Our disagreements often lead to the best outcomes because we challenge each other in a positive, constructive way. We push the limits of creativity and resilience, helping one another see the world—and opportunities—from a different angle. That tension becomes a source of growth. At the core of everything is love and deep respect. I always say Engy is like a daughter to me. For me, ANTY isn't just a business—it's a way to stay connected for life. It's something that bonds us, and one day will bond our children, too. Family is everything, and this brand is an extension of that love and connection.

You've spoken about uplifting other women and immigrant designers through collaborations. Can you tell us about one such collaboration that especially embodies ANTY's mission?

I've always been passionate about empowe-

ring women—I even worked at UN Women years ago because I deeply believe in that mission. At ANTY, we intentionally collaborate with women designers and especially welcome immigrant designers to reach out and work with us. One thing we make sure of is giving them full credit for their creations. We know how much women contribute—not just creatively but often as the backbone of their families. Fashion is still a male-dominated industry, but we're inspired by the rise of powerful female voices and are proud to play a part in opening more doors. That's what ANTY stands for.

Exploring 1940s Fashion

ASHLEY HASTY

Shares Her Literary Journey and the Intersection of Fashion History and Storytelling

By Beauty Prime Staff

Ashley Hasty is a remarkable force in both the literary and fashion education spheres, seamlessly blending these distinct fields into a cohesive narrative that captivates and educates. As the creative mind behind the widely acclaimed Hasty Book List, Ashley has transformed a simple Instagram hashtag into a renowned literary platform that now serves as a trusted resource for book enthusiasts worldwide. Her academic background in fashion history enriches her literary pursuits, adding layers of depth and authenticity to her work, especially in her ongoing historical fiction manuscript about 1940s fashion. Ashley's ability to infuse cultural narratives into her storytelling is a testament to her multi-faceted expertise and her dedication to both her craft and her audience.

At Mosaic Digest magazine, we are thrilled to feature an interview with Ashley, whose journey from academia to the online literary community exemplifies the power of storytelling across mediums. Her unique intersection of fashion, history, and literature not only enhances her writing but also inspires her readers to appreciate the myriad ways in which these disciplines connect. As an artist, writer, educator, and mother, Ashley's diverse roles offer rich perspectives that resonate throughout her interviews and book reviews. Her commitment to her community and her passion for literature make her an invaluable voice in the world of books and beyond. Mosaic Digest is proud to delve into the mind of a creator who continuously bridges the gap between past and present, history and modernity, through every project she undertakes.

Your upcoming historical fiction manuscript focuses on 1940s fashion. How has your extensive background in fashion history influenced the narrative and character development in your writing?

Before having a child, I wrote a manuscript. My background in fashion history allows me to weave authentic details into my storytelling, making the world of my manuscript feel immersive and true to the era. Fashion is never just about clothing—it reflects culture, identity, and even politics. In the 1940s, wartime restrictions influ-

enced everything from fabric choices to silhouette changes, and I use these elements to inform my characters' personal struggles and triumphs. The research process is one of my favorite parts of writing historical fiction, and my academic foundation helps me blend fact with fiction in a compelling way. However, since becoming a stay-at-home-mom, I've put this particular creative pursuit on hold. I do hope to return to it someday and hopefully get it published in the future. It is a story that needs to be told.

Transitioning from academia to blogging, how did your experience teaching fashion history and branding at Indiana University shape the content and direction of Hasty Book List?

Teaching fashion history and branding at Indiana University gave me a deep appreciation for storytelling—not just in books but in how people and brands communicate their identities. That understanding shaped the way I approached Hasty Book List, ensuring it wasn't just a place for book recommendations but a thoughtfully curated space where literature, history, and personal experience intersect. My academic experience also gave me confidence in research and

Ashley Hasty discusses her literary platform, passion for historical fiction and fashion history, and the integration of her diverse roles shaping her writing and creative pursuits.

analysis, which I apply when reviewing books and interviewing authors. Additionally, branding plays a key role in the success of any platform, and I leveraged that knowledge to make Hasty Book List a recognizable and trusted name in the literary community.

Hasty Book List started as a simple Instagram hashtag and has grown into a comprehensive literary platform. What were some pivotal moments that contributed to its evolution?

One of the first pivotal moments was when I expanded from Instagram posts to a full website. This allowed me to offer more in-depth reviews, interviews, and book lists beyond the constraints of social media. Another key moment was when authors and publishers began reaching out for features, which helped establish Hasty Book List as a respected literary platform. The biggest transformation, though, was embracing SEO

and the more administrative aspects of running a blog. When I recognized the blog could be more than a personal space and more of a resource to others, I opened this blog up to more readers. Each of these moments helped shape Hasty Book List into what it is today—a dynamic and multi-platform resource for book lovers.

As the curator behind "Hasty Book List", what unique perspectives do you bring to discussions, and how has this role enriched your engagement with the literary community?

Curating Hasty Book List has given me the opportunity to engage with literature from multiple angles—not just as a reader, but as an advocate for authors and a connector between books and their ideal audiences. My background in fashion history helps me appreciate how cultural narratives influence storytelling, and I bring that perspective into my discussions about books. Additionally, my experience as an educator means I approach literature with an analytical mindset, always looking for themes and deeper meanings that might resonate with readers. Running Hasty Book List has also expanded my literary community, allowing me to form meaningful relationships with authors, publishers, and fellow book lovers. It's incredibly fulfilling to create a space where books are celebrated and where readers can discover their next favorite story.

Balancing roles as a writer, artist, educator, and mother is no small feat. How do these diverse aspects of your life intersect and influence each other, both personally and professionally?

These roles are deeply intertwined, often in unexpected ways. My love for history and storytelling influences how I engage with my son, whether it's through reading together or exploring museums in Chicago. My artistic side helps me approach writing and blogging with creativity, and my background in education ensures that I remain curious and eager to learn. Parenthood has also reshaped my relationship with time—I've become more intentional with my creative pursuits, knowing that every moment is valuable. Ultimately, these roles feed into each other, making me a more well-rounded storyteller and a more mindful creator in all aspects of my work.

Hasty Book List is thrilled to collaborate with Friend of a Mom, a monthly Chicago dinner series that creates space for moms to connect, recharge, and feel seen. Together, we're launching a new book club designed specifically for Chicago moms—whether you're a devoted reader or just looking to rediscover the joy of reading after motherhood. With thoughtfully selected books, meaningful conversations, and cozy meetups over cocktails and community, this collaboration brings together the heart of Friend of a Mom's supportive gatherings and Hasty Book List's passion for connecting readers.

"

Fashion is never just about clothing—it reflects culture, identity, and even politics."

Ashley Hasty

Ashley Hasty, a dynamic writer and literary influencer, brings history to life through her storytelling and creative endeavors.

Beauty sleep is essential for skin regeneration and collagen production.

The Science of Beauty Sleep

Why Restful Nights Are the Key To Glowing Skin Health

By Beauty Prime Staff

This article explains how sleep helps repair and rejuvenate your skin, the effects of sleep deprivation on beauty, and how to create the perfect nighttime skincare and self-care routine for glowing results.

It's no secret that sleep is vital for your health, but did you know that it's also a critical component of your beauty routine? While you rest, your body undergoes a miraculous rejuvenation process that impacts everything from your complexion to your overall radiance. Beauty sleep isn't just a myth—it's the ultimate skincare strategy.

In this article, we delve into how sleep affects your skin, uncover the common pitfalls of sleep deprivation, and offer expert tips to enhance your bedtime routine for glowing results.

What Happens to Your Skin While You Sleep?

When your head hits the pillow, your body begins a complex repair and renewal process. During sleep, your skin cells regenerate at a higher rate, helping to repair damage caused by sun exposure, pollution, and other environmental stressors. Collagen production also ramps up, keeping your skin firm, elastic, and wrinkle-free.

Melatonin, the sleep hormone, plays a major role in protecting your skin against free radicals and ensuring optimal repair. Sleep is when your body truly works its wonders, delivering that fresh-faced glow we all crave.

What Sleep Deprivation Does to Your Skin

The occasional late-night Netflix binge or sleepless night out may leave you looking a bit tired, but consistent sleep deprivation can wreak havoc on your skin:

• **Increased cortisol levels:** Stress hormones rise with poor sleep, leading to inflammation, breakouts, and dullness.

• **Premature ageing:** Lack of sleep reduces collagen production and skin elasticity, resulting in early fine lines and wrinkles.

• **Dark circles and puffiness:** Stagnant blood flow under the eyes due to sleep deprivation causes the dreaded racoon-eyed look.

Investing in a solid sleep schedule is one of the most impactful ways to prevent these skin woes.

Continued *on page 40*

Continued *from page 39*

Sleep deprivation
increases stress
hormone levels,
leading to dullness,
wrinkles, and
inflammation.

Photo Credit: Photo by Kampus Production

The Role of Nighttime Skincare Products

Your skin works extra hard at night, making it the perfect time to layer on products that enhance its repair process. Incorporating the right skincare ingredients into your regimen can turbo-charge your beauty sleep:

• **Hyaluronic acid:** Locks in moisture to plump and hydrate skin overnight.

• **Antioxidants:** Combat free radicals and environmental damage.

• **Retinoids:** Stimulate collagen production to soften wrinkles and improve texture.

Choose lightweight moisturisers and serums that won't clog your pores to keep your skin breathing as you snooze.

Create the Perfect Pre-Bedtime Beauty Routine

Transform your evenings into a luxurious self-care ritual that benefits both your skin and your mind:

1. Cleanse: Rid your skin of makeup, oil, and dirt with a gentle cleanser.

2. Exfoliate (2-3 times per week): Remove dead skin cells for enhanced absorption of active ingredients.

3. Hydrate: Apply a hydrating serum or oil with ingredients like hyaluronic acid or squalane.

4. Moisturise: Seal in hydration with a nourishing night cream.

5. Eye treatment: Use a depuffing eye cream or mask to brighten tired eyes.

Pair this skincare routine with calming rituals such as dim lighting, relaxing herbal tea, or aromatherapy to prepare your mind for restful sleep.

Holistic Hacks for Better Sleep and Skin

True beauty sleep doesn't just stop at skincare. Adopting healthy habits can significantly enhance the quality of your snooze and, consequently, your skin:

- **Set a bedtime schedule:** Going to bed and waking up at the same time helps regulate your body's circadian rhythm.

- **Avoid late-night snacking:** Sugary or salty snacks can cause puffiness or skin inflammation.

- **Use silk pillowcases:** They create less friction for your skin and hair, preventing wrinkles and breakage.

- **Stay hydrated:** Proper hydration keeps your skin elastic and prevents dryness while you sleep.

- **Switch off screens:** Digital devices emit blue light that disrupts melatonin production—bad for both your sleep and your skin.

Continued *on page 41*

Continued *from page 40*

Fake It When Sleep Isn't On Your Side

Some nights, sleep may elude you, and that's OK. On those days, quick beauty hacks can help you appear well-rested and radiant:

1. Depuff your eyes: Use chilled cucumber slices or a cooling eye gel to reduce swelling.

2. Brighten your complexion: Apply a vitamin C serum for an instant glow.

3. Conceal dark circles: A colour-correcting concealer can banish under-eye shadows with ease.

4. Add life to your look: A touch of blush or highlighter can make your face appear fresh and awake.

With these tricks, you can easily fake a full night's sleep and keep your confidence intact.

Beauty sleep is more than just a saying—it's a cornerstone of your skincare. Treat your evenings as an opportunity to pamper yourself, allowing your skin and mind to recover and recharge. Prioritise restful nights and watch your skin transform into its best, most radiant version.

Ready to share your secrets? Join the conversation using BeautyPrimeSleepSecrets to showcase your nighttime beauty routine!

Your glowing skin awaits—start tonight!

> "Glowing skin begins with restful nights and the right nighttime skincare routine."

Photo Credit: Courtesy Of Simeart

"

Amber Guinness at
Arniano, her Tuscan
farmhouse, where her
passion for seasonal
cooking and slow liv-
ing comes to life.

Amber Guinness Brings Tuscany To Life

The Fusion Of Classical Techniques And Modern Vision

AMBER GUINNESS

On The Art Of Tuscan Winter Cooking

by Taste London Staff

Amber Guinness shares her love for Tuscan winter cuisine, blending traditional recipes, hidden gems, and the philosophy of "quanto basta" to inspire intuitive, unhurried cooking and cultural exploration.

Amber Guinness is a name synonymous with the rich tapestry of Tuscan cuisine and culture, a true ambassador of its winter comforts and culinary secrets. Born in London but rooted in the rolling hills of Tuscany, Amber's life at Arniano, the restored farmhouse near Siena, has shaped her into a storyteller of food, place, and tradition. Her work is a celebration of the Italian way of life, where instinct and simplicity reign supreme, and the philosophy of "quanto basta" — as much as you need — becomes a guiding principle for both cooking and living.

Her latest cookbook, *Winter in Tuscany*, is more than a collection of recipes; it is an invitation to slow down, to savour, and to immerse oneself in the rhythms of the season. Amber's writing evokes the warmth of a Tuscan kitchen, the aroma of simmering broths, and the artistry of dishes that elevate humble ingredients to something extraordinary. From the robust flavours of spaghetti all'ubriacona to the delicate comfort of mini malfatti in broth, her recipes are imbued with a sense of place and purpose, offering readers a taste of

Life & Food

Continued *on page 44*

Continued *from page 43*

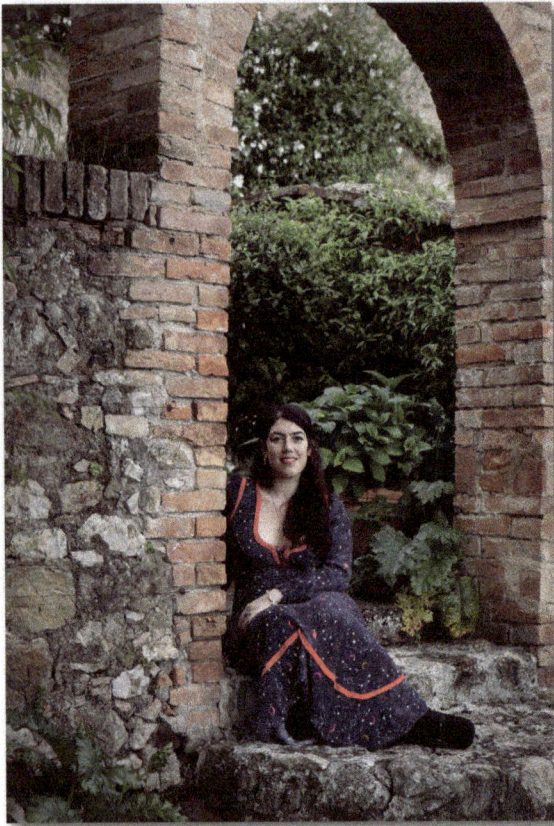

Amber Guinness with her son, crafting homemade pici pasta, a cherished winter activity at Arniano.

Tuscany's soul.

What sets Amber apart is her ability to intertwine her artistic sensibility with her culinary expertise. Her background as a painter infuses every page of her book with a visual richness, a reminder that food is not just sustenance but a form of beauty and expression. She guides us to hidden gems like Monte Oliveto Maggiore, where the monks' saffron speltotto embodies centuries of tradition, and to cosy trattorias where long, indulgent lunches are a way of life. Her approach to cooking is unhurried, reflective, and deeply connected to the land and its bounty.

Amber's work also challenges misconceptions about Tuscan cuisine, showcasing its vegetarian diversity and the central role of vegetables like cavolo nero. She brings authenticity to her recipes, often gleaned from cherished family traditions or the kitchens of beloved local restaurants. Her dedication to perfecting each dish, whether by watching nonna Anna stir her zuppa di farro or recreating the pillowy lightness of polpette al Limone, speaks to her passion for sharing Tuscany's culinary heritage.

In this interview, Amber Guinness invites us into her world — a world where cooking is an act of love, where food is a celebration of life, and where winter in Tuscany is a season of warmth, togetherness, and endless inspiration. Her words and recipes are a gift, reminding us to embrace the philosophy of "quanto basta" not just in the kitchen, but in all aspects of our lives. Amber Guinness is, without doubt, a beacon of Tuscan culinary artistry, and *Winter in Tuscany* is a testament to her enduring love affair with this enchanting region.

The "quanto basta" philosophy is central to your cookbook. Can you explain how this approach differs from traditional recipes and what benefits it offers home cooks?

The 'Q.B.' (quanto basta) approach represent so much of what I love about Italian cooking, these two letters illustrate in black and white that cooking a meal doesn't need to be an exacting affair if you use your instincts. It literally means 'as much as you need' and if you leaf through any cookbook originally written in Italian you'll see that in the list of ingredients for any recipes, many of them are followed by those initials. Basically, meaning you should add as much salt, flour, butter or oil, or whatever it might be, as is needed. It's an approach that encourages you to use your instincts rather

"Winter is a time for being cosy, hibernating, and hunkering down with a good meal."

than painstakingly measure out olive oil when a glug or two will do. Instead, if you add ingredients little by little and most importantly, taste as you go, then the quantities (within reason) don't matter too much and any 'mistakes' will usually be rectifiable. I love the sentiment behind it, that of not stressing too much or taking cooking too seriously, but instead of using your taste, touch, instinct and a little bit of common sense to make something tasty, which to me is a really wonderful philosophy for any home cook to remember.

Your book features many traditional Tuscan winter dishes. Which recipe are you most proud of, and why? What makes it particularly special or representative of Tuscan cuisine?

I really love the collection of recipes in this book. I love that there is something for every occasion and that many of the recipes elevate humble ingredients, scraps or cheaper cuts of meat to make something delicious for cold winter nights. One pasta dish that I'm particularly fond of is the spaghetti all'ubriacona (drunkard's spaghetti) which is an old recipe from Chianti, designed to use up the scarti - leftover wine that wasn't the best for drinking. I find it an unusual, interesting and very tasty recipe. The wine is cooked down in the pan with pancetta and onion until the alcohol has evaporated and spaghetti is cooked in a mixture of wine and water to impart some of the violet colour. The result is fabulous and has the added benefit of being a great recipe to use up that half drunk bottle of wine that's been sitting on the kitchen counter for two weeks.

"Winter in Tuscany" is more than just a cookbook; it's a journey through the region. What are some of your favorite hidden gems or lesser-known aspects of Tuscany that you share in the book?

Since I was a child living in Tuscany, my family's favourite cultural outing has always been going to visit the abbey of Monte Oliveto Maggiore. It's a beautiful working Benedictine monastery which sits in very lovely part of Tuscany called the Creti Senesi. The abbey is most famous for its cloister which is frescoed and depicts scenes from the life of St Benedict painted by Signorelli and Sodoma. The frescoes are spectacular and well worth a visit in the quieter winter months, when you may well have the place entirely to yourself. The monastery also has a beautiful church

Continued *on page 45*

Continued *from page 44*

with a famous wooden inlaid choir stand. Their working farm makes one of the best olive oils in Italy (it was once voted one of the top 40) and they produce honey, spelt, saffron and wine. The monks kindly shared their recipe for saffron speltotto, which they developed as a way of using all the amazing produce they grow on their farm (homegrown spelt, saffron, white wine and olive oil). A visit to the monastery can be combined with a delicious lunch at the neighbouring restaurant, La Torre, a short walk from the abbey. La Torre is a fabulous family run restaurant serving typical Sienese dishes such as pici, tagliatelle and, when in season, white truffles. They also serve the wonderful wines made by the monks of Monte Oliveto.

> *"Cooking a meal doesn't need to be an exacting affair if you use your instincts."*

Amber Guinness hosting guests at her Tuscan farmhouse, showcasing her passion for seasonal, slow-cooked meals.

You mention exploring Tuscany at a slower pace. How does this approach influence both the cooking and the overall experience described in the book?

I like doing everything more slowly in winter! It's a time for being cosy, hibernating and hunkering down with a good book, or even better, over a good meal. It's when I most relish being in the kitchen over a hot stove and not rushing, taking my time over the course of several hours to make broth, cook a peposo (black pepper stew) or make homemade pici with my son. When the nights draw in early, what better way to spend an afternoon? That's true of taking in culture as well and exploring new places, there is no point overstretching your itinerary to take in all the blockbuster sites, why not choose one or two lesser known gems, perhaps one for the morning and one for the afternoon - punctuated by a long, indulgent lunch in a cosy trattoria - and really take your time to walk around and take in the beauty.

Many of the recipes highlight specific Tuscan ingredients (cavolo nero, stracchino, etc.). Can you tell us about one ingredient that is particularly special to you and why it plays such an important role in Tuscan winter cooking?

Possibly the most emblematic of all Tuscan vegetables is cavolo nero, or 'black cabbage', a type of brassica with no head, instead growing in long elegant dark leaves, similar to kale. The leaves feel almost rubbery and need cooking to become edible. Growing rampantly from the autumn into the new

year in Tuscany, they are at their best when there has been a frost as the extreme cold tenderises the leaves. It's one of my favourite vegetables and has long been used in Tuscany during the winter months to stir though soups, such as ribollita, stir fried with chilli and garlic as a side dish or be blanched and whizzed into a delicious wintery pesto to dress pasta. There is a lovely recipe in the book which is a cavolo nero pasta with walnuts and pecorino which is very warming on a winter's night and makes one feel one is eating one's greens whilst also indulging in some pasta!

The book includes suggestions for local wines. Can you recommend a specific wine pairing for one of your favorite recipes in the book, and explain why they complement each other?

> *"The secret to the meatballs was to use cheap, white sliced bread soaked in milk."*

As a rule of thumb, more robust full bodied wines go better with robust meatier dishes, while lighter, more acidic wines go with lighter dishes, or with melted cheese to cut through the fat. If I were to have a Bistecca Fiorentina (Florentine t bone steak), the best pairing I could suggest would be a good brunello di Montalcino, my favourites are from Tenuta Buon Tempo and Castiglione del Bosco. However if I was having the baked fennel with pasta and bechamel from the book (one of my favourite recipes), I would opt for something less full bodied so that the wine and creamy bechamel sauce didn't over power each other, a good alternatice would be a Chianti Classico from Fonterutoli or a

Continued *on page 46*

Continued *from page 45*

Amber Guinness preparing a traditional Tuscan dish in her farmhouse kitchen, surrounded by the rustic charm of Arniano.

Roots of Renaissance: Patrick Faure's Surreal Tribute to Cosimo de Medici

> *"Tuscans are affectionally known in other parts of Italy as 'I mangi-afagioli' (the bean eaters)."*

Rosso di Montalcino, also from Tenuta Buon Tempo or Castiglione del Bosco.

You run a painting school in your home outside Florence. How does your artistic background influence your approach to cooking and presenting the recipes in "Winter in Tuscany"?

Well, I suppose it means that I mind about aesthetics! Which translates into my loving a beautifully laid table or presented dish. I love a colourful meal and a sense of balance in flavours, textures and colours when planning a menu.

What is the biggest misconception people have about Tuscan cuisine, and how does your book aim to correct that?

Probably the biggest misconception is that it is entirely meat based and while it definitely has 'meaty' elements – Bistecca Fiorentina, wild boar stews and ragus, ect. Tuscan cuisine also celebrates vegetables and pulses in a myriad of ways. To this day, Tuscans are affectionately known in other parts of Italy as 'I mangiafagioli' (the bean eaters) and many of Tuscany's famous soups and mainstay dishes are entirely vegan, being based around cannellini beans, chickpeas or spelt. Vegetables also play a central role, and cavolo nero, fennel, artichokes, radicchio, are all elevated to dizzying heights of deliciousness in winter. The fact that over half the recipes in this book are vegetarian highlights this. I've also included a chapter called 'Piatti di mezzo', meaning 'in between dishes' ie. Those which are vegetarian but don't quite fit into the 'Primi section of pasta and soup as they are too substantial, but also probably wouldn't classify as a 'secondo' as they aren't meat based or include pastry or an element of pasta.

What was the most challenging recipe to perfect for the book, and what lessons did you learn during the process?

There are two recipes in the book which are from two of my favourite restaurants in the world. One is the zuppa di farro - spelt and cannellini bean soup - which was always what I would order at Da Mario in Buonconvento if my dad took us there for lunch after school when I was a child and the other are the polpette al Limone - lemony meatballs -from Alla Vecchia Bettola in Florence. Both these restaurants very kindly shared their recipes with me, but the trouble was that there isn't really a recipe for

Continued *on page 47*

Amber Guinness at her Tuscan farmhouse, where cooking, creativity, and the "quanto basta" philosophy flourish amidst stunning landscapes and rich culinary traditions.

either, they are made in the restaurant kitchen the 'quanto basta' way, so they could only really describe the process rather than with any idea of quantities. In the end I had to go and actually watch both of these dishes being made as they weren't turning out in my kitchen as they tasted in the restaurant. After that everything fell into place and the soup became the comforting, creamy thick base with plump little pieces of spelt floating in it I had always eaten as a child and the meatballs became as light and pillowy as at the Vecchia Bettola. The secret the soup as it turned out was to cook the spelt separately to the soup itself and add it just before serving so it retained its delicious texture with a little bite - step seemingly so obvious to nonna Anna, the proprietress, she didn't think she needed to tell me when describing the cooking method to me. The secret to the meatballs was to use cheap, white sliced bread soaked in milk rather than breadcrumbs.

What's your favorite thing to cook from the book for yourself or your family on a cold winter's evening? What makes it so comforting?

Definitely Mama's mini malfatti in broth. Malfatti are ricotta and spinach dumplings, sort of like gnocchi, which you poach and normally dress in sage butter or tomato sauce (there is a recipe for these versions in my first book) but my mother would always make mini malfatti to poach and serve in homemade chicken broth in winter. It's so delicious, warming and comforting. There is something so lovely about when someone has taken the trouble to make homemade stock, to extract every last piece of goodness and flavour from a load of vegetables or meat. It's hands off but takes patience, so I really appreciate it when someone serves it to me and conversely I make it to show people I love them and to bring them comfort as I find any brothy soup comforting and nostalgic. Broth is also a lovely vehicle for lots of good things, mini malfatti or little pieces of pasta, vegetables or poached chicken

Masuma Zahara Bukhari Sparks Innovation with Sinsible Food's Plant-Based Masterpiece, Cardamom Sunset

Cardamom Sunset Redefines Wellness And Sustainability

Masuma Zahara Bukhari, founder of Sinsible Food, introduces Cardamom Sunset—a sustainable, plant-based drink merging health, tradition, and indulgence for premium spaces, showcasing innovative ingredients with sustainability and wellness at its core.

BY ePRIME STAFF | **LONDON**

Visionary innovation and unwavering dedication define Masuma Zahara Bukhari's journey as a pioneer in the plant-based beverage industry. As the founder of Sinsible Food Ltd., Masuma is steering the food and wellness market into uncharted territory with her ingenious creation, the Cardamom Sunset. This luxurious dairy-free drink, crafted with mindful simplicity and rooted in tradition, is an extraordinary testament to the power of combining health, sustainability, and indulgence in perfect harmony.

Masuma's passion for clean-label, plant-based nutrition stems from her own transformative experiences, and her ability to channel those into a product that resonates on a broader scale is remarkable. By meticulously selecting natural ingredients like Medjool dates, saffron, and cardamom for their flavour and health benefits, she has given life to a beverage that seamlessly unites functionality, sustainability, and a love for flavourful nourishment. Her commitment to mindful consumption, underscored by sustainable practices like refillable glass packaging and zero waste principles, is not only forward-thinking but an inspiring call to action for the food industry at large.

Cardamom Sunset is more than just a drink; it's a bold reimagining of what wellness-driven luxury can—and should—look like. We are proud to showcase the brilliance of Masuma Zahara Bukhari, a trailblazer whose entrepreneurial spirit and dedication to health and sustainability stand as an inspiration for current and future innovators alike. Read on to discover her journey, her values, and her vision for a better tomorrow.

What inspired you to create Sinsible Food and develop the Cardamom Sunset beverage? Was there a particular moment that sparked your entrepreneurial journey?

During my fitness journey, I decided to cut out dairy—but I deeply missed those thick, sweet milkshakes I used to love. I soon realised that those sugar-laden shakes and milk drinks were one of the main things holding me back from losing weight. That's when I began experimenting with natural ingredients I already had in my kitchen. The process made me stop and truly examine the packaged foods and drinks I was buying every week. Before long, I found myself immersed

Continued *on page 50*

"

Masuma Zahara Bukhari, founder of Sinsible Food, holding her revolutionary dairy-free drink, Cardamom Sunset, reflecting mindful luxury and innovation. Photos by Ilona Higgins.

SinSible

CHILLED PLANT SHAKE

CARDAMOM SUNSET

ORGANIC | VEGAN

A velvety, refreshing blend of rich almond & medjool dates, delicately infused with the exotic warmth of cardamom and saffron for a naturally satisfying indulgence.

100ml℮

Masuma Zahara Bukhari, visionary founder of Sinsible Food, proudly show-cases Cardamom Sunset—a plant-based, sustainable drink redefining luxury and mindful living.

> *"That's how Sinsible was born— creating drinks that nourish the body, satisfy cravings, and leave you feeling good, not guilty."*
> *– Bukhari*

in creating delicious, wholesome drinks that nourished my body, satisfied my cravings, and left me feeling good—not guilty. And that's how Sinsible was born.

Your beverage features unique ingredients like Medjool dates, saffron, and cardamom. How has your heritage influenced the flavours and concept of your product?

Medjool dates, saffron, cardamoms and nuts have always found their way into my kitchen, rooted in the complex and aromatic cooking traditions of my Asian heritage. Yet it wasn't until I started exploring their health benefits—and using them more intentionally— that I truly appreciated their functional effects.

During periods of fatigue or seasonal change, I began noticing how ingredients like cardamom, saffron, and dates helped balance my mood and sustain my energy through demanding workouts and daily routines.

I'll admit, I never used to enjoy eating dates on their own. But once I learned how nutrient-dense they are—rich in magnesium, fibre, and potassium—and discovered their naturally sweet, caramel-like flavour,

> *"Medjool dates… balance my mood and sustain energy through demanding workouts and daily routines."*
> *– Bukhari*

I saw them in a completely new light. Medjool dates, with their high antioxidant content, became a true staple in my recipes.

In our Cardamom Sunset drink, Medjool dates play a key role in delivering those nutrients, antioxidants, and minerals in a delicious, accessible way. Taking a step back to appreciate these natural ingredients has reshaped how I see the incredible resources available to us—and how we can nurture better eating habits for ourselves and the next generation.

You emphasise mindful living and sustainability in your brand. How do these values shape your product development and business decisions?

My product—and those to come—are an extension

Continued *on page 51*

Continued *from page 50*

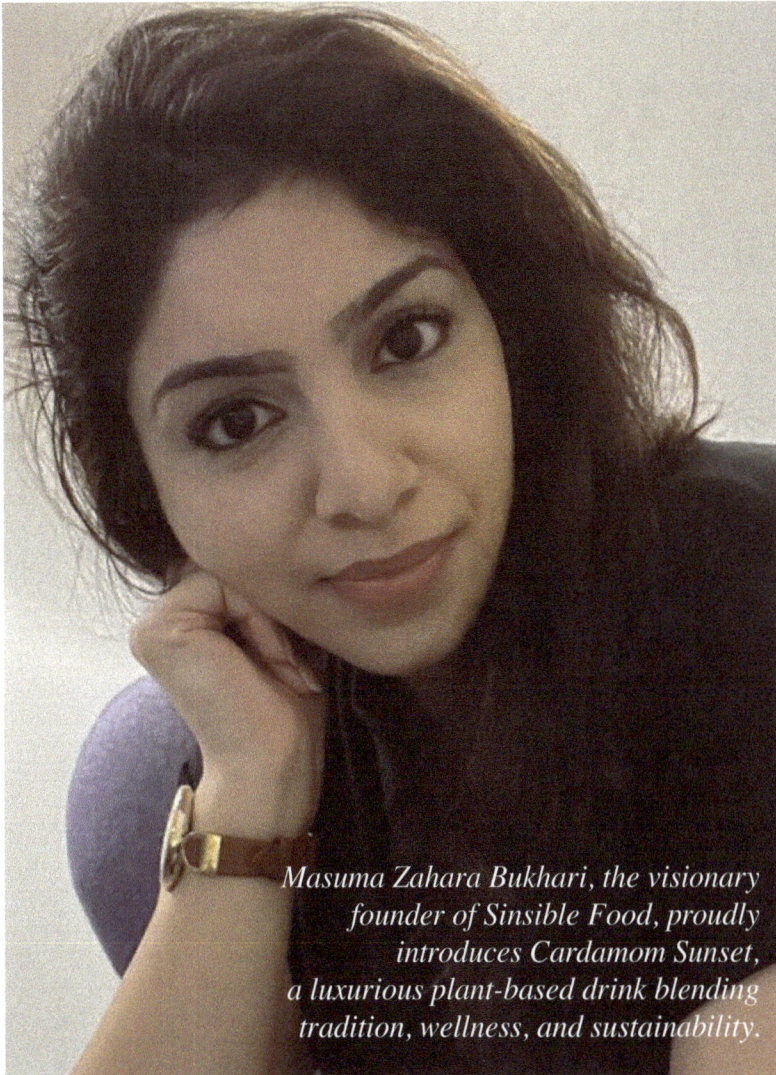

Masuma Zahara Bukhari, the visionary founder of Sinsible Food, proudly introduces Cardamom Sunset, a luxurious plant-based drink blending tradition, wellness, and sustainability.

you and your brand?

The Soil Association is a leading UK-based membership charity and the nation's largest organic certification body. Obtaining Organic certification through the Soil Association is an essential part of our brand's foundation. Ensuring that our company remains mindful and responsible toward the future is not only necessary, but also a commitment to the well-being of future generations.

It is important to me that our original intention remains at the heart of the brand: creating a giftable, luxorious, organic, plant-based drink that isn't packaged in a tetra pack. As we grow, this focus will not change. I would trust only the Soil Association to uphold and advocate for our organic status.

How does health and functionality play a role in the design of your drink, and what sets it apart from the existing plant-based beverages on the market?

The Sinsible Organic Vegan Cardamom Sunset Shake is designed with purpose— to energise, taste sinfully delicious, and remain completely sensible all at once. Every ingredient is chosen for its functional benefits; each one contributes to the shake's overall health profile. All the ingredients are rich in antioxidants and offer anti-inflammatory properties. What truly sets us apart is our commitment to sustainability. Our packaging is fully refillable and endlessly reusable. The glass bottles can be used over and over again—unlike plastic, they don't degrade—and we also incentivise bottle returns so the experience feels not only good, but genuinely rewarding.

We use whole Medjool dates in our formulation, which is extremely rare in the UK based on my research. I'm intentional and generous with every ingredient, even when they come at a high cost - "nothing is more costly than your health."

What advice would you offer to aspiring entrepreneurs hoping to launch their own food or beverage brand, particularly in the plant-based and wellness-focused space?

Continue to persevere and strengthen connections with fellow entrepreneurs; together, we can accomplish greater things.

---

of the values I've built into my own eating habits. I believe in mindful living, appreciating the resources available to us, and using ingredients responsibly. This includes making thoughtful food choices and sharing that knowledge with our children and the people around us.

I've woven these principles into Sinsible by sharing clear, factual information about the benefits of the ingredients we use, helping anyone who encounters our brand understand why those ingredients matter. When customers understand the value behind what they're consuming, I trust they'll make more mindful choices and carry that awareness forward—ultimately embracing the idea of being intentional about what they eat.

Sinsible champions healthy eating and respecting the earth that nourishes us. This is reflected in our circular system: purchasing and enjoying the shake, then returning the bottles for reuse. Sustainability is at the core of the Sinsible Cardamom Sunset, from our refillable and returnable glass packaging to the thoughtful use of by-products from our

ingredients. We operate as a circular brand, returning to the earth what belongs there— such as composted date pits and cardamom shells—while giving our glass bottles a new life through continuous reuse

What have been the biggest challenges you've faced in developing a clean-label, plant-based beverage within such a competitive industry?

The entire branding process has been a real challenge. Developing, formulating, and ensuring a drink is "safe" is a meticulous undertaking that demands focus, determination, and passion. This is my first time formulating a drink for commercial release, and the experience has given me a wealth of new skills and knowledge. From microbial and nutritional considerations to advertising and branding, it has been a comprehensive project—and one that I've genuinely enjoyed.

The Cardamom Sunset drink is currently pending organic certification. Why is achieving this certification important to

Nature, Family, and Second Chances

ASHLEY WESTON

Shares Her Journey of Dreams, Family, and Faith Through Compelling Storytelling

EDITOR'S DESK | LONDON

Ashley Weston, an ingenious storyteller hailing from Gilbert, AZ, brings to life narratives that resonate deeply with readers, capturing themes of healing, forgiveness, and unwavering hope. With a spirit rooted in faith and family, Ashley's delightful novels unfold emotions that inspire, encouraging her audience to dream while making them swoon through the art of storytelling. From the moment she penned her first story as a third-grader, Ashley realized her passion for writing was intertwined with her life experiences—an odyssey that transformed her dreams into reality, fueled by relentless support and deep personal insights.

At Mosaic Digest magazine, we are thrilled to illuminate Ashley's literary journey as she delves into her distinct style of narrative. Her "Marlow's Boys Ranch" series is not merely fiction; it is infused with authenticity drawn from real places and profound experiences. Ashley's work is a testament to the influence of her childhood, outdoor healing spaces, and the steadfast love of family. Her novels promote the transformative power of second chances and forgiveness, inviting readers to explore complex characters who navigate life's moral dilemmas with grace—a reflection of Ashley's own beliefs.

Balancing motherhood with a writing career, Ashley nurtures her four children while crafting stories during moments stolen from her daily life. She illustrates the hopes of better world-building through narratives infused with love and familial values—a dedication mirrored in her effort to touch the hearts of her readers, especially those grappling with chronic illnesses. Indeed, the candid feedback and heartfelt interactions with her readership bring validation to her mission, driving Ashley to continue influencing and uplifting lives with each written word.

Mosaic Digest magazine celebrates Ashley's dedication to create compassionate stories that foster connection and empathy.

Her life and work exemplify the essence of genuine storytelling—reminding us that, even amidst struggles, faith and hope offer boundless possibilities.

Your novels often explore themes of healing and personal growth. How have your own experiences with chronic illness influenced the emotional depth and authenticity of your storytelling?

Dealing with constant pain starting as a young child is not the easiest thing to navigate. I used to spend a lot of time alone and one of the ways I would cope with that loneliness would be to write. Journal my thoughts and feelings, and eventually that turned into story-telling. For me, it's so important to help others feel seen and to know they aren't alone as I was for so many years. If I could portray that in any small way into my stories, I feel like I've done my job, and maybe there's a bigger reason as to why I suffered with it than just for me.

Ashley Weston discusses her novels' themes of healing, forgiveness, family, and faith, drawing on her personal experiences to uplift readers through storytelling.

In your "Marlow's Boys Ranch" series, you delve into the dynamics of found families and second chances. What inspired you to set these narratives in a ranch setting, and how does this environment enhance the stories you aim to tell?

Growing up I spent every summer at my grandma's cousin's cabin in Colorado on land. Everything written in my series is based on real people and a real place. I've always wanted to influence youth and help them feel a little less alone in the world, and by creating a safe place for them that struggle, that was important to me. This ranch, though fictional in a sense of being a boy's ranch for healing, was based on a place I often found healing in for myself. Being outside is grounding and healing. Seeing

the same two elderly family members who brought a consistent love and kindness to me each summer was so important for how I viewed the external world. Nature and family in a consistent manner is quite powerful to an adolescent.

I also believe in the power of forgiveness, and second chances is a perfect way to relay that in this type of setting. If we can forgive others for "doing wrong", we can also forgive ourselves. It's an ever evolving cycle.

Balancing a writing career with motherhood to four children is no small feat. Can you share how your family life shapes your writing process and the themes you choose to explore in your books?

I'm very blessed to have a supportive husband who, if I ask, gives me time to write. But I honestly try my best to show up for my family, they come first, so I tend to write during nap times or after bedtime when they don't need me. I don't want to miss out on their growth. I hope to write stories, though romance infused, with hope and healing to be an example to my children. If we can help our children be better adults, the world will be a better place.

Faith appears to be a significant aspect of your life. How does your spirituality influence the characters you create and the moral dilemmas they face within your stories?

This one is a little more tricky because it tends to be where a lot of opinions arise in readership. Some people love faith-based stories and some don't. I try my best to not focus solely on one aspect of faith to make it more multidimensional with other's beliefs but at the end of the day, my faith is who I am and a part of me, and that will trickle into my stories. With faith comes hope, and with hope anything is possible. Isn't that what we all want? Happy endings and the possibility that anything can happen?

I want to portray real life scenarios of people who struggle, but with the aspect that faith and/or hope helps us to fight through the struggle. Not just suffer through it.

With all of that, there is always a sense of right and wrong, and a moral compass to my characters. I think we are mostly born with those instincts and I want to remind others that once again, they are not alone in those feelings. It's okay to feel a pull, and to make decisions with consequences attached. Good or bad.

You've mentioned a desire to help readers feel less alone through your writing. Could you discuss a particular reader interaction or feedback that affirmed this mission and perhaps influenced your subsequent work?

I honestly worried that no one would care to read this book because it isn't the normal storyline with tropes and banter. But I've had several women with chronic illness, or with someone they know who has suffered from it, reach out to me and tell me how much they appreciated me being vulnerable enough to write this story. How it helped them to feel understood. How it gave them a chance to feel like the leading role in a story. To me, that is EVERYTHING. That is what keeps me writing.

Renowned Author Ashley Weston: Crafting Heartfelt Narratives with Hope, Faith, and Family

"

To me, that is EVERYTHING. That is what keeps me writing."

Ashley Weston

Amanda Walcott: The inspiring young founder behind Beachside Bikinis, redefining swimwear with sustainable designs and meaningful customer experiences.

Amanda Walcott Proves Beachside Bikinis Is More Than Just Swimwear

A Young Entrepreneur Redefining Swimwear With Purpose And Passion

Amanda Walcott, founder of Beachside Bikinis, shares her journey of resilience, creating sustainable swimwear, and building a meaningful brand that champions ethical production and individuality, all at just seventeen years old.

By Lyra Green

Amanda Walcott is, without a doubt, a force to be reckoned with. At just seventeen years of age, Amanda has channelled the challenges of her personal journey into a remarkable entrepreneurial venture that speaks volumes about her creativity, determination, and eye for innovation. After enduring a difficult year of health setbacks and self-discovery, this young visionary has emerged not only as a beacon of resilience but also as the founder of Beachside Bikinis—a brand that is redefining swimwear with its sustainable ethos and carefully curated designs.

What sets Amanda apart is her ability to turn adversity into opportunity. Her experience revealed not just a gap in the swimwear market for petite and selectively crafted styles but also inspired a brand steeped in purpose and passion. Beachside Bikinis isn't merely about fashion—it's an extension of Amanda's values and her commitment to ethical production and sustainability. Every detail, from the cut of the fabric to the personal touches in packaging, reflects Amanda's unwavering dedication to making both the product and the experience meaningful for her customers.

Amanda's innovative approach, coupled with her mature perspective on business, is a testament to how passion, when fuelled by purpose, can create something truly extraordinary. Her story is as inspiring as the mission behind her brand, and we are thrilled to highlight this remarkable young entrepreneur in the pages of Beauty Prime. Prepare to be inspired, as Amanda's vision for Beachside Bikinis proves that age is no barrier to ambition, and challenges can indeed be the foundation for change.

Amanda Walcott's creativity, determination, and commitment to sustainability exemplify how passion and values can drive meaningful business success.

Continued *on page 56*

Amanda Walcott radiates confidence as she builds a brand rooted in sustainability, ethical practices, and thoughtful designs.

"Sustainability is important to me because nature keeps us healthy, so it is our job to keep nature healthy."
– Amanda Walcott

What inspired you to focus so heavily on sustainability and ethical production with Beachside Bikinis?

Sustainability is important to me because nature keeps us healthy, so it is our job to keep nature healthy. Running a business can cause a lot of damage to the planet, so I try my best to minimize our eco-footprint. Ethical production matters to me because it is the only morally right way to go about production. All people deserve safe, fair, and respectable working conditions. I believe in treating people with kindness and respect, and when something comes from a place of love, it shows. It is important to me that Beachside Bikinis are made from a place of love, positive intentions, and morals.

How do you select and design the limited styles and cuts you offer, and what makes them unique compared to other brands?

First, I select my favorite styles, evaluate why I like them, and consider what could be improved upon/changed. Each of the chosen styles go through layers of design, sampling, and consideration - leading to the final measurements, angles, and details. All of the variations (colors, fabrics etc.) have been thoughtfully designed for a cut, allowing them to embrace a single identity. Beachside Bikinis are selective, comfortable, high quality, fashion forward, sustainable and ethical. Our swimwear features subtle and elegant branding, closer size scaling (smaller), soft fabrics, and remarkable consideration. By focusing on one target market, we have the ability to create more tailored products, as

Continued *on page 57*

well as a simple, straightforward shopping experience.

Can you walk us through how your personal recovery experience influenced the mission and values of Beachside Bikinis?

My journey has led me to evolve and grow as a human being, entrepreneur, designer, and creative. The BB mission is to make the world a better place, one little thing at a time. Experiencing what I did really inspired me to notice "the little things" in life. It shaped my knowledge for what I needed to create, and how I want to impact and inspire others.

What challenges did you face launching a brand at such a young age, especially after going through a major health setback?

The biggest challenge that I have faced creating a brand at 15 and launching at 16 is believing in myself. I have struggled with being able to push past the belief that a business can't be taken seriously because I am young, or that someone else knows better. I have grown so much with this company, and am proud to be able to trust my own opinion versus seeking reassurance from others.

What does the customer experience mean to you, and how do you ensure that every Beachside Bikinis package delivers on your vision of a "wrapped up experience"?

The customer experience is a top priority and we aim to create the best: from the shopping, receiving, wearing, and loving of Beachside Bikinis. Our straightforward shopping experience aims to be an easy, enjoyable task. I carefully package everything personally, and always have the goal to make someone's day (at least a little better). The product bags have "BB" quotes on them, the tags have qr codes for the customer's easy access, and I like to write handwritten notes to the customer (sometimes with a discount/coupon code). Lastly, we hope that our customers make the best memories and enjoy their time wearing Beachside Bikinis ●

Beachside Bikinis

The visionary behind Beachside Bikinis, Amanda Walcott, combines creativity and conscience to craft swim

"
Eunice Opoku, the visionary founder of viemaa, dedicated to transforming beauty with innovation and inclusivity.

Eunice Opoku Leads a Revolutionary Movement with viemaa to Empower and Transform the Beauty Industry

Redefining Beauty Through Empowerment, Inclusivity, and Cultural Connection

Eunice Opoku discusses viemaa's mission to empower through inclusive, sustainable hair care, celebrating identity and emotional connections worldwide hair rituals.

By Ember Wilson

Eunice Opoku is a name that resonates with vision, innovation, and unwavering purpose. A true trailblazer in the health and beauty aids industry, she has dedicated over two decades to creating products that are as meaningful as they are revolutionary. As someone who has not only built brands but also redefined what modern beauty can stand for, Opoku has made it her mission to ensure that every product she touches empowers individuals, celebrates diversity, and honours the deeply personal rituals tied to self-care.

From her remarkable tenure leading high-performing consumer product strategies in global markets to her transformative work as founder of WAMHJO Group LLC, Eunice has consistently exemplified the power of combining strategy with soul. Her latest venture, viemaa, is no exception. This premium hair care brand is far more than a collection of products—it's a powerful movement rooted in empowerment, inclusivity, and giving back. Built on the pillars of innovation and cultural authenticity, viemaa addresses the often overlooked emotional and identity-driven connection to hair while pioneering high-performance, sustainable beauty.

What sets Opoku apart is the profound intentionality with which she approaches her work. Whether developing products for underserved communities, giving back through the "Save A Strand, Save A Soul™" initiative, or challenging Eurocentric norms within the beauty industry, Eunice leads with empathy and cultural fluency. Her inspiring philosophy, "beauty shouldn't ask you to change who you are; it should help you become more of who you've always been," encapsulates the ethos of viemaa and the heart of its groundbreaking work.

Eunice's ability to transform personal pain points and global observations into a brand that uplifts and inspires is nothing short of extraordinary. In this exclusive interview, Beauty Prime has the privilege of delving into Eunice Opoku's world—a world where hair is celebrated as a powerful symbol of identity and transformation, and where meaningful, scalable change begins one strand at a time. We are honoured to share her insights, passion, and vision in this issue, and we hope you find her story as empowering and transformative as we have.

What personal experiences or challenges in your global travels most directly inspired you to create viemaa?

viemaa was born from a simple but powerful truth: hair isn't just hair. It's identity. It's expression. **It's power. It's you.**

During my travels across Southeast Asia, the Middle East, Africa, Europe and Latin America, I saw firsthand how personal and sacred hair care is for women around the wor-

> *"We build differently—because we've had to live in a system that wasn't built for us."*
> **– Eunice Opoku**

Continued *on page* 60

Eunice's philosophy:

"Beauty shouldn't ask you to change who you are; it should help you embrace yourself."

Continued *from page 59*

> "Beauty shouldn't ask you to change who you are; it should help you become more of who you've always been."
> – Eunice Opoku

ld. Despite vastly different cultures, one thing remained constant women were deeply connected to their hair. Many were using time-honored traditions and natural remedies passed down through generations, even as they struggled to find modern products that supported their unique hair needs.

What struck me most was the emotional disconnect between those rituals and the products available in the market. So many women—especially those with textured, curly, or coily hair—were adapting their routines to fit beauty systems that didn't include them. The global beauty industry was still pushing formulas designed around Eurocentric standards, offering harsh, drying products that prioritized aesthetics over actual hair health.

I understood the frustration intimately. For years, I used mainstream products that were not made for my hair. I dealt with dryness, breakage, and damage, constantly chasing solutions that didn't exist. It took time—and a lot of unlearning—to realize the problem wasn't my hair.

It was the products.

But what truly inspired viemaa were the women I met who, despite these challenges, were still finding ways to care for themselves. Women who blended oils in their kitchens, who treated wash day like a sacred ritual, who turned hair care into self-care. Their resilience, creativity, and connection to heritage moved me deeply.

That's when I envisioned viemaa: a brand rooted in science, powered by innovation and driven by impact. A brand that doesn't just make hair care—but makes space for identity, self-love, and empowerment.

At viemaa, we believe that when you care for your hair with intention, you're not just following a routine—you're practicing a ritual. A moment of self-connection. A form of self-respect. Every element of our brand—from our ingredients to our packaging to our product names—is designed to uplift, affirm, and inspire.

Each product is named with purpose. We

Continued *on page 61*

Continued *from page 60*

Products cater to diverse hair textures with scientifically backed, plant-powered formulas.

call them "Affirmations for Your Strands." Names like "Self-Esteemed Strengthener BOND SHAMPOO" and "Confidence Cocktail DAILY STYLING SERUM" turn your daily routine into a personal mantra—a quiet moment of power at the start or end of your day. It's about giving women the confidence to show up as their boldest, most authentic selves.

This is self-love, strand by strand.

This is viemaa.

What started as a personal pain point and a global observation turned into a movement— one that honors the emotional and cultural significance of hair while delivering innovative, high-performance care for every texture. In a world where so many still feel pressured to conform, viemaa invites you to connect. To embrace. To rise.

Because beauty shouldn't ask you to change who you are. It should help you become more of who you've always been.

How did you ensure that viemaa's products would be truly inclusive and meet the diverse hair care needs you observed around the world?

"True inclusivity isn't just about who's in the campaign—it's about who's in the lab and on the testing panel." **– Eunice Opoku**

We built viemaa with diversity at the core. That meant starting with a global testing community—across all hair types, climates, and routines—and partnering with experts in textured and multicultural hair care. Our products are pH-balanced, silicone-free, and formulated with nutrient-rich, plant-powered ingredients that cater to a wide range of needs.

Inclusivity, for us, is not about fitting everyone into the same mold. It's about offering flexible, science-backed products that support each person's unique hair journey—whether natural, treated, curly, or straight.

viemaa emphasizes both high performance and sustainability—what were some of the biggest challenges you faced balancing these two priorities during product development?

"We had to resist the industry's shortcuts— because great hair shouldn't come at the planet's expense." **– Eunice Opoku**

The hardest part was refusing to compromise on either value. Many high-performance ingredients are petroleum-based or environmentally harmful. So, we sourced cleaner, plant-based alternatives and partnered with ethical suppliers—even when it cost more or took longer.

Our bottles are recyclable, and we've removed silicones and parabens from our formulations. We also had to reeducate consumers true product performance is about long-term hair health and environmental care.

Continued *on page 62*

Products cater to diverse hair textures with scientifically backed, plant-powered formulas.

Continued *from page 61*

Can you share more about the philosophy behind "Save A Strand, Save A Soul" and how viemaa connects beauty with social impact?

Absolutely. "Save A Strand, Save A Soul" is more than a mission statement—it's the heart of everything we do at viemaa. We believe that hair care is emotional, not just cosmetic. Hair holds weight. It's a thread that ties us to our identity, our culture, our memories—and sometimes, even our pain.

We've met women who lost their hair due to illness or trauma, and the moment they begin to nurture it again, you can see something awaken in them.

"When someone reclaims their hair, they often reclaim a piece of themselves."
– Eunice Opoku

Beauty, for us, isn't about perfection—it's about restoration. It's a pathway to dignity, resilience, and meaningful change. That's why a portion of every viemaa purchase supports women and children in underprivileged communities. We provide free hair care products, self-care resources, and emotional support to help them reconnect with themselves—starting from the roots, quite literally.

We like to say we're making a difference one strand at a time. And we truly believe that when you heal the person in the mirror, you begin to heal so much more than what's visible.

As a women-owned, minority-owned brand, what unique perspectives do you think viemaa brings to the beauty industry?

"We build differently—because we've had to live in a system that wasn't built for us."
– Eunice Opoku

Our perspective is shaped by exclusion, resilience, and the determination to create something better—not just for ourselves, but for everyone who's ever felt unseen in the beauty space.

We bring the lived experiences of those historically left out—not only from boardrooms, but from product shelves and marketing campaigns. viemaa reflects the voices, textures, and stories that mainstream beauty has often overlooked. We lead with empathy,

intentionality, and cultural fluency—not because it's trendy, but because it's who we are. We prioritize science, innovation, community, and equity—not just trends.

Being a minority- and women-owned brand means we're not here to fill a market gap—we're here to ask why that gap existed in the first place.

We're not replicating old systems. We're reshaping them. We're redefining what luxury, innovation, and representation look like. And representation is not performative—it's deeply personal.

We're proud to be reforming what beauty looks like, what power sounds like, and most importantly, who gets to be centered in the conversation.

Looking ahead, how do you envision viemaa continuing to evolve and expand its mission of empowering individuals through hair care and self-expression?

"Hair is our medium—but empowerment is our mission." **– Eunice Opoku**

The future of viemaa is more than product collections or market share—it's about shaping a beauty landscape that reflects real people, real needs, and real stories. That's why we launched the viemaa tribe, a growing community dedicated to connection, education, and self-expression.

We see viemaa growing in both size and influence. That means expanding our reach—but also expanding our impact. As a brand rooted in empowerment, we don't just want to participate in the beauty industry—we want to help lead it. We want to set trends, elevate standards, and be a voice in shaping the future of beauty, especially for underrepresented communities.

A major focus for us moving forward is deeper personalization. Everyone's hair journey is unique, and the one-size-fits-all approach simply doesn't work. That's why we're investing in innovation—developing tools and technology that allow users to build custom routines based on their hair type, lifestyle, and even environment. Our goal is to make smart, tailored hair care both accessible and inclusive.

We're also expanding our product offerings—starting with scalp health. Healthy hair begins at the root, so we're creating solutions that support the scalp microbiome, address

stress-related conditions, and nourish from within. This new category allows us to take a more holistic approach, bridging beauty with overall wellness.

As we grow, we're staying deeply committed to our values. viemaa is proud to be a women-owned, minority-owned, and WBENC-certified brand. That certification isn't just symbolic—it's a tool for creating access. It helps us build supplier diversity, foster meaningful corporate partnerships, and support other women and minority entrepreneurs along the way.

But growth for us isn't just external. Education will continue to be central to our mission—especially when it comes to reshaping the cultural narrative around hair. For too long, hair care has been framed as maintenance or control. We want to rewrite that narrative and reframe hair care as celebration.

Through workshops, digital content, and community activations, we aim to empower the next generation with knowledge, pride, and the confidence to embrace their natural texture and heritage. Whether it's a tween learning their first twist-out or a woman reconnecting with her roots after years of chemical treatments, we want to be there—offering guidance, encouragement, and real solutions.

As viemaa evolves, so does our storytelling. We're committed to showing the real, diverse, beautiful spectrum of identity—across cultures, genders, generations, and textures. Hair is a language of self-expression, and our job is to make sure everyone has the tools and freedom to speak fluently in that language.

At its core, viemaa has always been about more than beautiful hair. Our mission is to empower individuals through intentional rituals and affirming products that help them reconnect—with themselves, their roots, and their communities.

So, as we scale, we'll stay grounded in purpose:

To create beauty that's clean, conscious, and culturally relevant.

To innovate boldly, while honoring tradition.

To empower, strand by strand.

Because hair is our medium—but empowerment is our mission●

The Art of Belonging with Sun You

How spontaneity and care animate Sun You's sculptures and panels

Sun You *explores themes of impermanence, domesticity nostalgia, using humble materials in her art. She discusses how movement between cultures shapes her creative process and curatorial projects.*

Sun You's art embraces both resilience and fragility, transforming everyday materials into vibrant reflections on connection, memory interdependence.

Sun You's art offers a compelling meditation on themes of impermanence, interdependence play, bringing together the deeply personal with the universally relatable. Born in Seoul and based in New York, You has built an impressive body of work that transforms everyday materials like polymer clay and cardboard into intricate sculptures and wall pieces. Her thoughtful approach celebrates the beauty of fragility, creating pieces that evoke both lightness and resilience. Recognized with accolades such as the 2023 Contemporary Visual Art Award from the AHL Foundation, You's impact extends beyond her art. As a professor, curator director of President Clinton Projects, she is dedicated to fostering collaborative and supportive communities for artists.

Sun You discusses how her life between Seoul, Detroit New York has shaped her art, revealing the intimate themes of domesticity, nostalgia adaptation woven into her work. Her perspective brings fresh insight into the way movement, memory creative spontaneity guide her artistic practice, inviting viewers to reflect on their own experiences of home, transformation connection.

How has your experience of moving between different cities like Seoul, Detroit New York influenced your artistic process and the themes you explore in your work?

In my life, I have moved and traveled a lot. This fluidity and impermanence have influenced how I think and create. I prioritize flexibility and lightness. My work does not require fixed production sites, as it can be easily packed and made spontaneously.

How does the idea of function and arrangement in your process of packing art for transport contribute to the meaning of your sculptures?

My floor sculptures, made from polymer clay and cardboard boxes, have been exhibited since 2021. The form of these sculptures arises from a process in my work. I bake clay pieces in the kitchen oven and pack them in boxes to move to the studio. The arrangement of the clay is based on function: I organize them so they won't shift or break in transit. Whereas the paintings are composed with concerns like balance or movement, the compositions in the boxes come from a place of caretaking. There is a directness to this that I want to celebrate.

In your practice, you incorporate materials that are often associated with childhood and play, such as polymer clay. How do you see the relationship between these materials and the themes of domesticity and nostalgia in your work?

My abstract panels function as both paintings and wall reliefs. These works are made with polymer clay, acrylic paint wood. Polymer clay, one of my primary materials, is typically used in crafts such as bead making and children's play. The association with domesticity and baking in my work is reinforced through hand-building techniques, including rolling, pinching firing clay in my home oven.

For my show at Sardine in 2018, I created multi-panel paintings that are stacked on top of each other, with sculptural pieces inserted between the paintings. Both elements reflect a playful language reminiscent of children's play.

Several artists have inspired you. How do you think your artistic style and philosophy align or contrast with theirs?

I admire many artists, including B. Wurtz—we both use humble materials, embracing a slow, sublime succinct approach to gesture. I also admire Polly Apfelbaum, as we both are interested in creating provisional tableaus that celebrate women's work, history of craft the language of abstraction.

Can you elaborate on your thoughts about impermanence and interdependence, especially in the context of the current social climate and how it informs your artistic practice?

Impermanence and interdependence aren't ideas to me—they're facts. As a person, I try to embrace this and, as an artist, to materialize it. Some of the ways I do this include sculptures that are held together in precarious arrangements using magnets and gravity. Each time they're displayed, they shift and change.

As a curator, how do you choose the themes and artists for your projects what do you hope to communicate through these exhibitions?

My curatorial projects are often an extension of my interests as an artist and individual. These include themes such as artist migration and gentrification, feminism, physical flexibility in sculpture, intergenerational inspiration among artists more. These shows and events have been essential in fostering conversations and relationships that continue to shape my growth as an artist and educator. My goal is to bring people together, expand connections build community through artist-initiated exhibitions, projects curatorial opportunities.

The Brisley Bell: A picture-perfect Norfolk retreat with award-winning gardens, exquisite dining, and warm country charm.

Outstanding Opulence At The Brisley Bell

Where Norfolk's Heritage Meets Modern Hospitality

The Brisley Bell is more than just an enchanting Norfolk pub—it's a celebration of community, heritage, and vision, brought to life under the extraordinary leadership of Amelia Nicholson. As co-owner, Amelia's remarkable journey through creative industries, from theatre to antiques, has shaped the soul of this award-winning inn in deeply meaningful ways. Mosaic Digest is thrilled to feature Amelia and her endeavours in this exclusive interview, where we explore the story behind The Brisley Bell's transformation into a boutique haven that seamlessly blends rustic charm with contemporary elegance.

Amelia's artistry and eye for detail are evident in every corner of the inn—from the thoughtful interiors that welcome guests with warmth to the carefully crafted pub gardens recognized as some of the finest in the UK. Her background in directing and producing adds a layer of ingenuity and storytelling that elevates The Bell far beyond its beautiful exterior, creating an experience that resonates long after the visit.

Joined in stewardship by Marcus Seaman, whose farming roots and entrepreneurial spirit bring a deep understanding of rural hospitality, and Chef Hervé Stouvenel, a culinary master with Michelin training, The Brisley Bell champions the best of Norfolk. Whether it's showcasing hyper-local ingredients, nurturing partnerships with regional producers, or creating spaces where history and modernity coexist in perfect harmony, Amelia and her team make an indelible mark on the inn's legacy and the surrounding community.

At NewYox Media, we celebrate creators

"We were determined that every space in our pub would be equally inviting."
– Amelia Nicholson

Amelia Nicholson and her team at The Brisley Bell transform a 17th-century inn Amelia's creativity, vision, and attention to detail make her a pioneer in blending artistry and hospitality at The Brisley Bell. <u>Photos by Nathan Neeve</u>

Amelia Nicholson and her team at The Brisley Bell transform a 17th-century inn into a stunning destination blending hospitality, heritage, and heart.

who weave their passions into spaces that delight, inspire, and sustain—and Amelia Nicholson embodies that ethos beautifully. In this interview, she generously shares the journey, challenges, and vision behind The Brisley Bell, offering words of wisdom and glimpses into the heart that beats behind their success.

What inspired you both to take on the challenge of restoring a 17th-century inn into such a thriving destination?

We were both seeking a change in career and decided to pool our resources. In all honesty, we weren't looking to work in hospitality, we were looking for a challenge, a project, but it could have been in any industry. We both used to drink at the pub when we were younger - and lived locally - when it happened to come up for sale. It had been left derelict for four years, which was such a shame, and we really needed somewhere new to eat in the area as there was very little choice. Our business plan made sense… so we took the plunge. It was an amazing, creative time!

Could you tell us about the process of blending the inn's traditional rustic features with contemporary design elements?

In the 80's and 90's many pubs extended their restaurant space without much thought

of how the new spaces connected to the old. The result was often lifeless rooms that lacked atmosphere. We were determined that every space in our pub would be equally inviting, so we took time to integrate old and new. It was also unaffordable to kit the pub out entirely in quality traditional wooden furniture and panelling, so we had to design our way out of this problem, which then inspired the modern elements.

The gardens are regarded as some of the finest pub gardens in the UK. What vision or ideas shaped their transformation?

Our vision was to design a space that invited guests to explore and relax, where every path or seating area offered something to discover. From the start, we imagined a shared space that encouraged people to slow down - a place to sit, linger, talk and feel at home. We didn't wish for it to resemble a commercial garden; rather, to evoke the charm of a garden belonging to a rural country home.

We wanted the garden to be as much of a draw as the pub itself - not just a backdrop, but a space guests would actively enjoy whilst being practical to the pubs needs. Being inland in Norfolk, we knew we needed to be unique to stand out and saw the potential to create a destination garden that felt just as layered, welcoming, and considered as our food and interiors.

How important is working with local

A beautifully plated gourmet dish featuring a golden pastry filled with creamy topping, garnished with vibrant edible flowers and fresh greens, served on a rustic wooden table in an inviting dining setting.

farms and suppliers in crafting the restaurants seasonally led menu?

It's vital - both to support the local economy and to build trusted relationships while reducing our carbon footprint. It's far more rewarding to work with suppliers we can meet, visit, and collaborate with directly. A seasonally led menu just makes sense; Marcus comes from a farming family, Norfolk is a farming county with some of the best soil in the country, and we're surrounded by exceptional local produce.

We also forage ourselves - for samphire on the marshes or buckets of apples, cherries, pears, and even quail eggs gifted by locals with bumper crops. There's a lovely full-circle synergy when we serve guests dishes created by Hervé, using the produce they have shared with us.

The Brisley Bell combines boutique luxury with the relaxed feel of a pub. How do you strike the right balance between these two elements?

The hardest balance is managing guests' expectations, as the beauty of being a freehold, independent venue means our offering is like no other. Some guests may be expecting a reception desk or room service, and others delight in how spacious and quiet the rooms are for a pub. What we can guarantee is an authentic welcome. We're earthy and agricultural but we do everything with care, passion and attention to detail - and that's where the luxury comes in!

What makes Chef Hervé Stouvenel's approach to cuisine so unique, and how does his Michelin training influence the dining experience?

Hervé brings a calm precision and deep respect for ingredients that stems from his Michelin training. His cooking is refined but never fussy - he understands balance and lets flavours speak for themselves. He's equally comfortable preparing a classic French sauce as he is creating a British Sunday roast and

A stunning culinary display at The Brisley Bell featuring artfully plated dishes of locally sourced ingredients, showcasing refined flavours and rustic charm against a cozy and elegant backdrop.

his versatility keeps our menu exciting and grounded in both skill and seasonality.

Do you feel a responsibility to reflect and champion the heritage of The Brisley Bell and if so, how do you achieve this?

Absolutely! We're just custodians in a long line of landlords since 1706. We feel very strongly that pubs are a part of British culture that need to be nurtured. The British 'do' pubs brilliantly and that's something to celebrate, particularly in rural areas where they are often the hub of the community.

Since opening, we've taken part in and documented national celebrations, and we've researched and published the pub's history on our website (after earlier records were sadly lost in a fire). We keep contributing to that story - for instance, a local painting group led by Country Life cartoonist, Annie Tempest, spent a year painting locals, and their portraits now hang on our walls. We're also tagging over 30 trees we planted in the garden, recording their species and planting dates for future generations.

Amelia, does your experience as a the-atre director influence the way you create an enjoyable and memorable experience for visitors?

I suppose it may. In theatre, the best productions often appear effortless, yet every detail has been carefully considered. A shared experience should resonate long after it's over, and that's true for hospitality too. It's all in the detail. Marcus and Hervé share that belief, and I think that's what makes us such a great team.

Marcus, how has your farming background shaped your outlook on running the inn and its restaurant in such a rural setting?

Farming teaches patience, practicality, and respect for the land, all qualities that translate directly to running a rural foodie pub. You learn to work with the seasons rather than against them, to value good produce. It's also a reminder that hard work and care over time yield real rewards - whether you're tending a field or running a business.

A Journey From Page To Screen

Pamela Callow Unveils The Intrigue Behind Her Bestselling Kate Lange Thriller Series

New York Times bestselling author Pamela Callow shares the inspiration, legal expertise, and research behind her Kate Lange series, exploring complexities of humanity through gripping narratives and suspenseful plots.

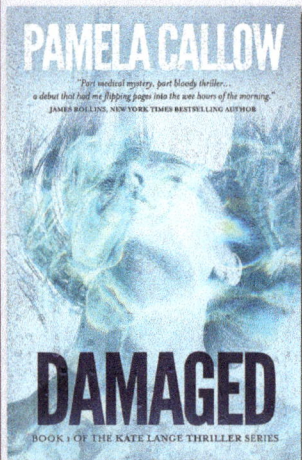

"DAMAGED" by Pamela Callow captivates with its thrilling blend of legal drama and chilling suspense. Kate Lange, a determined lawyer, finds herself entangled in a deadly conspiracy while confronting past traumas. Grippingly fast-paced, Callow's debut keeps readers burning the midnight oil, eagerly flipping pages to uncover dark secrets and relentless action.

BY EDITOR'S DESK | LONDON

Pamela Callow stands as an emblem of compelling storytelling in the world of crime fiction. With a knack for intertwining intellectual depth with emotional fortitude, her bestselling Kate Lange Thriller Series has captivated over a million readers, earning accolades comparable to giants like Robin Cook, Michael Crichton, and John Grisham. Her narratives, rooted in her profound understanding of the legal world, create an engaging tapestry of suspense and legal intrigue–offering readers a unique perspective that both fascinates and challenges the norms of the thriller genre.

Callow's ability to weave intricate plots with real-world legal drama has propelled her books to bestseller lists across North America and beyond, with translations spreading her gripping tales to international audiences in six countries. Her talent shines through innovative narratives like the celebrated Damaged and the thought-provoking Tattooed, keeping readers on the edge of their seats with a narrative pace akin to a roller-coaster ride.

Beyond the written word, Pamela Callow's endeavors into television adaptations of her work further cement her status as a multifaceted storyteller, bringing her vivid narratives to life on screen. Her collaboration with television producers on projects like the Arthur C. Clarke Venus Prime series demonstrates her adaptability and visionary approach to storytelling—a hallmark of her illustrious career.

As she continues to work on the eagerly anticipated Inflicted, the fifth installment of the Kate Lange series, readers and viewers alike can expect nothing short of electrifying suspense coupled with poignant reflections on society and justice. Mosaic Digest magazine is honored to feature an exclusive interview with Pamela Callow, a true luminary in the thriller genre whose works not only entertain but also enrich the understanding of human complexity through crime and resolution.

Your Kate Lange series has been praised for its gripping suspense and legal intrigue. What inspired you to create Kate, and how does your background in law influence your storytelling?

When I created the character of Kate Lange, I wanted to create a protagonist who didn't possess the usual crime solving skills. Instead, I created an ambitious but haunted woman who must rely on her wits and confront her demons in the pursuit of truth and justice.

My background in law and policy permeates my series. Like Kate, I was a junior lawyer in an elite law firm, with no previous connections to the legal world. I then switched careers after completing a Master's in Public Administration, and became a strategy consultant in an international consulting firm. Kate's world is one with which I'm very familiar—a blue chip corporate environment seething with hidden agendas and private ambitions. My legal training comes into play with every case Kate investigates, as I extensively research the law before I create my own cases for the series.

In Damaged (Book One), Kate becomes the hot potato in a power play between the new Managing Partner and his ousted rival. As Kate fights for her place in her firm, her make-or-break-case leads her to uncover a conspiracy (inspired by an actual criminal case)—and puts her in the path of a serial killer.

In Indefensible, Managing Partner Randall Barrett is accused of murder—and his estranged son is the only witness. The inspiration for this story came as a law student wondering what it would be like to be accused of a terrible crime.

Tattooed (Book Three), examines the right to an assisted death, while exploring the question of whether someone who can create beautiful art is capable of evil. And thus, celebrity tattoo artist Kenzie Sloane—and Kate's high school nemesis—was born.

Finally, in Exploited (Book Four), the question of whether private justice for the public good is examined in a case where a famous politician shoots an intruder, and Kate must defend her now-unconscious client only to try to stop a devious cyber plot.

Legal thrillers require a deep understanding of both the legal system and high-stakes drama. How do you balance accuracy with the need to keep readers on the edge of their seats?

It's a fine balance. It's important to me to be as accurate as possible, because that's how I roll. Also, because I strive for accuracy, it gives me special access to subject matter experts who trust that I will try to accurately represent their professions. This research gives me the basis of the cases and characters in each novel.

But being accurate doesn't mean the pace has to be slow. It means that the cases are rooted in reality, and the characters are authentic. Although the wheels of justice do indeed turn slowly, it's the crime that drives the pace. I make the timeline very short—usually about two weeks—in each of my books. The motivations and evidence are revealed through different characters' points of view, propelling the story forward. The result is a fast-paced, page-turning read in which I relentlessly ramp up the pace to a thrilling climax at the end.

Your books have been compared to bestsellers in the thriller genre. What do you think sets your storytelling apart, and what elements do you believe make a thriller truly unforgettable?

Quite simply, I think the appeal of my books is that they combine intellect with heart. I am a student of life. I share my characters' deepest secrets with my readers: their vulnerabilities and fears, their mistakes and hubris, their strengths and flaws. And then I immerse these characters—and the readers—in a complex world where a crime has rent the fabric of their lives.

Truly unforgettable thrillers possess page-turning suspense. Suspense is created by caring about the characters. I think we all see ourselves in some facet of them. But there's

also the converse—the question of Nietzsche's monster in the abyss. When we look into the abyss, do we see ourselves? Unforgettable thrillers make us think about the moral grey areas that we confront every day in our lives, the choices that are made, and the ripple effect they have on society.

Writing crime fiction often means diving into dark and intense themes. What is your approach to research, and how do you ensure authenticity without getting overwhelmed by the weight of the subject matter?

I conduct extensive research by reading cases, memoirs, technical documents. I then interview subject matter experts, including police detectives, forensic pathologists, forensic anthropologists, forensic identification experts, psychologists, etc. It's one of the fun aspects of my job!

But even though my novels are crime thrillers, I don't believe in sensationalizing violence. There is a raison d'être for every character (including a serial killer), and for every action in every book. I try to counteract intense themes by showing the personal lives of my characters—they are messy and human, just like us. Kate has a rescue husky who likes to leave a (toilet) paper trail.

Also, I think of myself as an "accidental thriller writer," as I'm quite optimistic by nature. So even though the themes can be weighty, at the end of the day, my books are hopeful.

Your novels have captivated a wide audience. What has been the most rewarding moment of your writing career so far, and what can readers expect from you next?

It was pretty amazing when my debut novel Damaged was selected as a Levy Home Entertainment "Need to Read" Pick, and hit the Nielsen Bookscan bestseller list on its release. Since then, I've sold over 350,000 print copies and reached over one million readers, hitting numerous e-book bestseller lists. But the most rewarding part of my work is that so many people around the world relate to the characters I create and the stories I tell.

In terms of what's next, I've been working on the development of the Kate Lange Thriller Series with a TV producer. I'm also trying to get the fifth Kate Lange book written, as I'm excited to share this story!

Pamela Callow, bestselling author of the Kate Lange Thriller Series, brings legal drama and suspense to life with remarkable skill.

"

My legal training comes into play with every case Kate investigates."

Pamela Callow
NEW YORK TIMES BEST-SELLING AUTHOR

Yoga A Timeless Path To Harmony And Self-Discovery

Embracing Yoga For Physical Wellness, Mental Clarity, And Spiritual Growth

Yoga, a practice with roots in ancient India, unites mind, body, and spirit, offering physical strength, emotional well-being, and spiritual growth for a more mindful and harmonious life.

In a world that often feels chaotic and fast-paced, yoga stands as a timeless sanctuary—a practice that has nurtured humanity for thousands of years. Originating in ancient India, yoga has transcended cultural and geographical boundaries to become a global phe- nomenon. This holistic discipline of- fers much more than physical exercise;it is a pathway to harony, mindfulness and self-discovery.

THE ESSENCE OF YOGA

At its core, yoga is a union—a connection between the mind, body, and spirit. Derived from the Sanskrit word "yuj," meaning to yoke or unite, yoga integrates breathing techniques (pranayama), physical postures (asanas), and meditation to create a balanced lifestyle. It is not merely a workout but a way of life that fosters inner peace and resilience.

PHYSICAL BENEFITS

Yoga is renowned for its ability to enhance physical health. Regular practice improves flexibility, strength, and posture. Asanas like downward dog, warrior pose, and tree pose engage multiple muscle groups, promoting overall fitness. Moreover, yoga can alleviate chronic pain, boost immunity, and sup-

port cardiovascular health. The gentle yet profound movements make it accessible to individuals of all ages and fitness levels.

MENTAL CLARITY AND EMOTIONAL WELL-BEING

In a world filled with distractions, yoga offers a space to quiet the mind and cultivate mindfulness. Focused breathing and meditation practices reduce stress, anxiety, and depression, fostering emotional stability. Yoga encourages self-awareness, helping practitioners navigate life's challenges with grace and equanimity.

SPIRITUAL AWAKENING

Beyond the physical and mental realms, yoga delves into the spiritual. It invites individuals to explore their inner selves, connecting with their true nature. Practices like mantra chanting, visualization, and deep meditation awaken a sense of purpose and unity with the universe.

YOGA FOR EVERYONE

One of the most beautiful aspects of yoga is its inclusivity. Whether you're a seasoned practitioner or a beginner, yoga adapts to meet your needs. From gentle restorative yoga to dynamic vinyasa flows, there's a style for everyone. It's not about perfection but about showing up for yourself, one breath at a time.

INCORPORATING YOGA INTO DAILY LIFE

You don't need a yoga mat or a dedicated studio to embrace this practice. Simple acts like mindful breathing, body stretches, or a few moments of meditation can seamlessly integrate yoga into your daily routine. Start small, and let the practice evolve organically.

Yoga is more than a trend; it's a timeless gift to humanity. It empowers individuals to lead healthier, more mindful lives while fostering a deep connection with themselves and the world around them. Whether you're seeking physical strength, mental clarity, or spiritual growth, yoga offers a transformative journey. So, roll out your mat, take a deep breath, and embark on this beautiful path of self-discovery. Namaste.

Yoga: A Timeless Practice
That Awakens The Body,
Mind, And Spirit.

Kristen Martin

Kristen Martin discusses writing across genres, transformative personal growth, spiritual awakening, career-defining moments, and her exciting upcoming projects, showcasing her passion for storytelling and empowering creatives.

Kristen Martin, a powerhouse of creativity and determination, is truly an inspiration in the literary and entrepreneurial worlds. As an Amazon bestselling author, writing coach, content creator, and speaker, Kristen has carved a remarkable path that merges storytelling with personal growth, ambition, and authenticity. With an impressive catalog spanning over ten books across genres like YA fantasy, science fiction, and personal development, her ability to create captivating narratives and introspective explorations is nothing short of extraordinary. Each page Kristen writes is infused with unshakable passion, boundless imagination, and a deep understanding of human connection—a trio that has solidified her work as a beacon of inspiration for readers around the globe.

In this feature, we delve into Kristen's creative journey and celebrate the brilliance behind her storytelling. From the intricate twists and turns of the *Shadow Crown* series to the deeply transformative experiences encapsulated in her self-help book *Soulflow*, Kristen's work demonstrates a rare versatility that transcends genres and inspires profound reflection. Whether she's immersing her readers into otherworldly realms or sharing her own heartfelt truths, her stories resonate deeply, leaving an indelible mark on readers' lives.

Beyond the pages, Kristen's role as a writing coach and creative entrepreneur showcases her commitment to empowering others to chase their dreams and unlock their own creative potential. Her YouTube and podcast platforms are shining examples of how she merges authenticity and expertise, motivating her audience to take bold strides toward living a life they love.

Mosaic Digest is proud to host this illuminating interview with Kristen, reflecting on her astonishing career, her evolutionary creative process, and her plans for what's next. Whether you're a writer seeking inspiration, a devoted fan of Kristen's work, or simply a lover of compelling storytelling, her insights offer an unforgettable glimpse into a mind brimming with creativity.

Exploring Genres, Personal Growth And Creative Evolution

Kristen Martin Inspires Through Storytelling and Creativity

Midnight Reign brings the Shadow Crown series to a dramatic conclusion. What was the most challenging part of wrapping up such an expansive story?

The most challenging part of writing the final book in the Shadow Crown series was making sure the conclusion had that final "punch" I'd been working up to for so many years. Of course, it's crucial to make sure any and all foreshadowing is wrapped up so that the reader isn't left wondering with more questions than answers. But, overall, writing an ending that was not only satisfying but worthwhile was the most challenging part of wrapping up this story.

During the process of writing your self-help book, Soulflow, what was one discovery that deeply impacted you or changed your perspective?

The depth of self-reflection shocked me. Soulflow forced me to confront my darkest shadows and deepest fears and write about them in what would become a very public medium. Vulnerability has never been my strong suit, but it was such a cathartic process that I actually cried while writing the entire ending of that book. Needless to say, it left me forever changed.

Your standalone novel Beyond the Stars and Shadows blends metaphysical elements with a contemporary setting—what inspired you to tell your story through this unique lens?

During the time of writing Beyond the Stars and Shadows, I was in the midst of a spiritual awakening. The pull I felt to capture my experiences through a creative outlet was so strong that I began mapping out characters to symbolize what I was going through. It's such an introspective story, one that was written during a pivotal moment of my life, and I'm so glad I was able to convey my journey through that unique lens.

Looking back on your journey as an author, coach, and entrepreneur, what moment or milestone stands out as the most defining in your career?

There are honestly so many, but if I had to pick just one, it would be attending BookCon during my book tour across the U.S. I had the opportunity to meet so many readers and fans, and feeling that sense of community, connection, and shared love of reading and writing is something I'll carry with me for the rest of my life.

As you continue to grow creatively and professionally, what new directions or projects are you most excited to pursue next?

I have a few manuscripts in the works. One is an urban fantasy with paranormal elements, another is a YA romantic fantasy, and the other is a gothic thriller, which is a new genre I'm just now dabbling in. As for content creation, I plan to continue documenting my creative process and lifestyle in the hopes that it will inspire writers from all walks of life to write their books and get their voice out there.

JoAnn M. Dickinson

*Multi-Award-Winning Author **JoAnn M. Dickinson,** known for her captivating children's books, celebrates storytelling that sparks imagination and lifelong learning.*

JoAnn M. Dickinson is a celebrated author whose children's books inspire and educate young readers by blending captivating adventures with meaningful life lessons. Her stories, often drawing from experiences with her grandchildren, explore themes like kindness, compassion, empathy, diversity, and the wonders of nature. With a focus on STEM, social-emotional learning (SEL), and auditory engagement, JoAnn's books help spark curiosity while nurturing a sense of self-discovery and learning in children.

We sat down with JoAnn to learn more about her creative journey and the impact her work has had on families around the world.

From Dream to Reality

JoAnn's journey as an author began with a moment of simple inspiration. "It all started with my grandson's first camping trip," she shares. "Witnessing his excitement and wonder as he explored nature motivated me to write *John's Camping Adventures*. It began as a simple story to capture that experience but grew into a passion I hadn't anticipated."

This pivotal moment not only launched JoAnn's first book but also set the course for a career in self-publishing. "I chose self-publishing to retain creative freedom and bring my stories to life on my timeline," she explains. Alongside a trusted team of editors, illustrators, and designers, JoAnn has built a body of work deeply rooted in creativity and intentionality. "Over time, my storytelling has become more purposeful, tackling themes like kindness, adventure, and STEM learning in ways that resonate with children."

The Inspiration Behind the Stories

JoAnn's most recent book, *Rory's Quest: A Lou's Zoo Adventure, i*s the third installment in her popular *Lou's Zoo Series*. "This book follows the heartfelt journey of Rory, a young rhino searching for his lost mother," she shares. "Rory faces challenges, relies on friends, and discovers the strength within himself. His story is about perseverance, hope, and the importance of meaningful connections."

Inspires Young Minds Through Enchanting Tales of Adventure and Learning

Celebrating Her Journey As A Multi-Award-Winning Children's Author

Through Rory's journey, JoAnn aims to leave a lasting message with her readers. "I hope families take away the power of resilience and the value of leaning on others for support, especially when facing life's unexpected challenges," she says.

Navigating Creativity and Business

As both an author and entrepreneur, JoAnn has faced the delicate balance of creativity and business. "The biggest challenge is dividing my time between writing and managing the ongoing demands of marketing," she explains. "While I love the creative process, I also need to promote my books, maintain a social media presence, attend book fairs, and connect with readers."

Although demanding, JoAnn has embraced this part of her career. "I've learned to prioritize my schedule and rely on my team when needed. The process has made me more resourceful and adaptable, and it's rewarding to see my stories reach children all over the world."

Encouraging Positivity and Learning

A hallmark of JoAnn's work is her focus on positivity, kindness, and enthusiasm for learning. "These are values I deeply believe in, and I incorporate them into my books natural-

ly," she says. "But beyond that, I'm passionate about making science and nature exciting for children. My *Amelia Ophelia Series,* for example, introduces kids to topics like bee conservation and ocean protection in fun, approachable ways."

For JoAnn, storytelling is about more than entertainment. "I want children to feel empowered—to see how their curiosity and actions can make a difference. In today's fast-paced, tech-centric world, stories that nurture empathy and education are more important than ever."

Connecting with Readers

One of JoAnn's greatest joys is hearing from young readers and their families. "I've had kids tell me they've been inspired to go camping like John or dream of building rockets like Rylee," she shares with a smile. "It's these moments of connection that remind me why I write."

Feedback from her readers also influences her work. "I pay attention to the questions kids ask or the characters they relate to most. Their excitement often fuels my next idea. At the heart of it, my goal is to create stories that make every child feel seen, inspired, and encouraged to explore their potential."

Bringing Scotland's Wild Beauty To Life

S. J. BARRATT

Inspires Young Minds With Eco-Adventures Fueled By Myth, Science And Her Love Of Nature

BY DAN PETERS | LONDON

S. J. Barratt stands as a remarkable force in contemporary children's literature, weaving together threads of ecology, adventure, and myth into tales that both educate and enchant. Based in the picturesque surroundings of Lyon, France, Barratt's life is deeply rooted in sustainable agriculture—a passion that unmistakably infuses her writing with authenticity and a respect for the natural world. Her award-winning series, Living at the Edge of the World, captivates middle-grade readers with its compelling settings, diverse stories, and heartfelt themes—all underscored by her meticulous research and dedication to environmental storytelling.

In this interview, we have the immense pleasure of sharing an illuminating interview with Barratt. Her eco-fiction series, set amidst Scotland's storied landscapes, has not only charmed reviewers but also garnered accolades such as the Silver Medal at BookFest 2024 for diversity in children's books and recognition from the Literary Titan. Her debut novel, Winter, brought forward the enduring ethos of Shetland's crofting culture, while its sequel, Spring, delved deeper into archaeology and Viking legend, leaving readers eager for the upcoming instalment, Summer.

From her exploration of social media's impact through her twin protagonists—Tabitha and Timothy—to her nuanced approach to fostering environmental education in young minds, Barratt's work is both timely and timeless. Her stories encourage readers to see the intricate beauty of the world around them, to tread more lightly upon it, and to embrace curiosity as a driving force for wonder and wisdom. As she prepares to unveil the third chapter of her series, featuring themes of ocean pollution and Selkie legends, we can only expect her narrative tapestry to grow richer still.

Through her words, Barratt demonstrates an unwavering belief in the transformative power of stories—blurring boundaries between cultures, landscapes, and the realms of science and myth. It is an honour to spotlight her voice in this issue and to offer our readers a glimpse into the creative mind behind these extraordinary tales.

How did your experience researching crofting and Shetland's landscapes shape the setting and themes in Living at the Edge of the World – Winter & Spring?

Having worked in agriculture for over 20 years, there are so many aspects of rural life I'd love young readers—and their parents—to better understand. I knew from the start that I wanted the story to be set on a farm, and crofting in Scotland felt like the perfect fit: small-scale, family-run, and deeply rooted in both community and the land.

When I came across Shetland, especially the island of Foula—with its population of just 30 people—I was captivated. It was the ideal backdrop to explore themes of isolation, resilience, and identity. The stark contrast between this remote, rustic way of life and the world of a wannabe influencer from trendy North London gave me a compelling framework for both tension and humor.

S. J. Barratt discusses eco-fiction, Viking legends, social dynamics, and cultural identity in her award-winning Living at the Edge of the World series, blending adventure, education, and environmental themes for middle-grade readers.

Winter garnered awards in 2024—how did recognition influence your approach to Spring, published March 20, 2025?

Winning my first award—a Silver Medal at BookFest—was such a thrill that I proudly featured it on Winter's cover. It gave me a real confidence boost and reinforced that the themes I was exploring resonated with readers.

When writing Spring, I felt encouraged to keep pushing myself creatively while staying true to the heart of the story. I've submitted it to a range of awards, including the North Street Book Prize, which offers valuable feedback—even if you don't win. That insight is invaluable to me.

The awards Winter received confirmed there's an appetite for stories that reflect both cultural diversity and unique landscapes. It's helped shape my direction going forward:

• Silver Medalist, BookFest 2024 — Children's Books: Diversity & Multicultural

• Bronze Medalist, Global Book Awards 2024 — Geography & Culture

• Finalist, Children's Book Excellence Awards 2025

Spring has since received a children's literature award from Literary Titan.

In Spring, the twins uncover a Viking artefact—what inspired you to weave archaeology and legend into a story for ages 9–12?

Many themes in my stories are grounded in real-life events. A few years ago, an islander in Foula digging for peat unearthed woollen fabric dating back to the Vikings. It wasn't a dramatic helmet or sword, but it sparked my imagination. I expanded on that and added a fictional twist to make it exciting for young readers.

I also wove in a simple soil experiment using cotton, to show how organic material breaks down over time—hands-on science that kids can try themselves. Combining real-world science with Norse legend made the writing process fun and educational—even for me!

The contrast between Tabitha's social-media mindset and Timothy's love of nature offers sharp character arcs—how did you develop that sibling dynamic?

I've always loved the dynamic between twins—so similar, yet so different. Tabitha is all about online validation and influencer dreams, while Timothy—"Wiki-Tim"—is grounded in curiosity and nature. His love of facts lets me bring in real information without it feeling forced—if I do it right!

I enjoy engaging with my own online community, but nothing restores the soul like a walk in nature, and I wanted that message to come through. Tabitha's journey isn't about judging social media, but about discovering that face-to-face connection and time outdoors can be even more fulfilling.

Your eco-fiction highlights agro-ecology and peat-bog conservation—how important is environmental education in your storytelling?

Very! I wanted readers to better understand how farming can work with nature. Agro-ecology is all about balance—especially important in crofting, where every bit of land counts. And peatbogs are amazing carbon sinks, so protecting them is crucial.

That said, if you live beside one, cutting peat for heating might still be more sustainable than importing fuel. In Spring, the twins are learning to cut peat when they stumble on the Viking helmet. It was a great opportunity to blend environmental education with adventure.

You're based in France but write about Shetland—how does living abroad affect your connection to Papala and its culture?

Having lived in France for longer than I did in Britain, I often feel caught between cultures—which naturally finds its way into my writing. The sense of not fully belonging is something I explore through Papala's characters and their varied backgrounds. In Winter, the twins—newcomers to the island—meet a Syrian boy, and together they navigate what it means to be different.

I've visited Shetland and Scotland many times and have established a lovely correspondence with a ranger from Foula, who generously reviews my drafts—especially the wildlife and farming details I rely on.

In your Q&A you mention "forcing yourself to write" through writer's block—what's your current writing routine while working on Summer?

I don't really believe in writer's block. I see it more as something to push through by simply getting words on the page. You can rewrite anything—but not a blank page.

I've finished the first draft of Summer, the third book, and I'm giving it some space before editing. I write best in the mornings, usually early when the house is quiet—or even propped up in bed with my laptop before the day begins. It might sound lazy, but it works for me!

Summer explores ocean pollution and the myths of the Selkies—those half-seal, half-human sea folk from Scottish legend. I'm aiming for publication next summer, with time set aside for self-editing, beta readers, professional feedback, and of course illustration work with the talented Jenny Nutbourne.

What one piece of advice would you give aspiring middle-grade authors hoping to blend adventure, ecology, and myth in children's literature?

Let curiosity lead the way. Research deeply, reach out to experts, and stay open to inspiration—whether it comes from a scientific article, a legend, or a single photo. The more curious you are, the richer and more meaningful your story will become.

S. J. Barratt, award-winning storyteller, blending myth, nature, and eco-fiction to inspire young readers through her *Living at the Edge of the World* series.

"

Research deeply, reach out to experts, and stay open to inspiration—curiosity can transform any story into something truly meaningful."

S. J. Barratt

UNTITLED (SELF-PORTRAIT)
by *Linda Karshan*

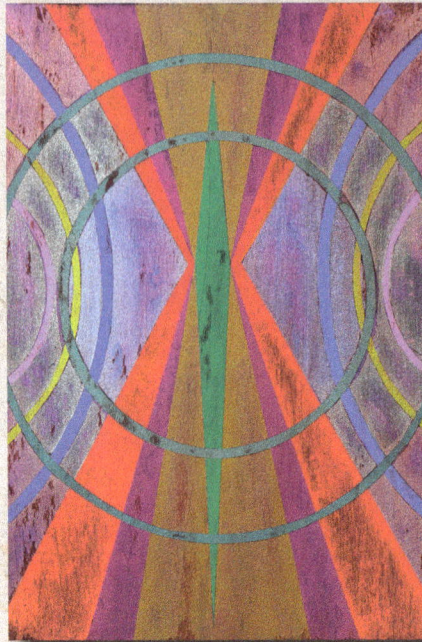

A SECRET LANDSCAPE
by *Bettina Weiß*

WOMAN IN RED II
by *Elise Ansel*

A masterful blend of precision and intuition, *Untitled (Self-portrait)* captures timeless rhythm, introspection and profound artistic depth.

Linda Karshan's *Untitled (Self-portrait)* (1994), part of The British Museum's collection, exemplifies her performance-based artistic method, where creation becomes a physical and meditative act. This work distills movement, rhythm and structure into a deceptively simple yet evocative composition, reflecting Karshan's philosophy that art emerges from the interplay of body, mind and time. Each mark on the page serves as a record of her "inner choreography."

The minimalist aesthetic of the piece belies its complexity. Composed of intersecting lines and geometric forms, it reflects Karshan's disciplined yet organic approach to mark-making. Her process—turning the paper counter-clockwise, rhythmic counting and deliberate bodily movements—is embedded in the work, creating a sense of balance and order reminiscent of Plato's theory of numerical harmony. The grid-like structure of vertical and horizontal lines is not just a visual element but a manifestation of her physical engagement with the medium. Each line carries purpose, as if echoing a universal rhythm.

What makes *Untitled (Self-portrait)* particularly compelling is its duality of precision and spontaneity. Grounded in geometric rigor, the work retains a sense of fluidity and openness, inviting viewers to interpret its meaning through their own lens. Its lack of overt representation allows it to function as a mirror, reflecting the viewer's thoughts while offering insight into the artist's introspective process.

Karshan's background in psychology and her engagement with D.W. Winnicott's theories of transitional space are evident here. The drawing exists in a liminal space between control and freedom, consciousness and the unconscious. It embodies creative play, a concept central to Winnicott's ideas, where making art becomes a dialogue between artist and medium. This interplay gives the work its vitality and depth.

In *Untitled (Self-portrait)*, Karshan achieves a rare synthesis of intellectual rigor and intuitive expression. The piece transcends traditional self-portraiture, becoming a portrait of her process, philosophy and connection to larger forces of time and space. Its simplicity and depth reward close observation, revealing new layers of meaning with each encounter. This work stands as a testament to Karshan's unique contribution to contemporary art.

Bettina Weiß's artwork masterfully blends geometry, color and texture, creating vibrant, thought-provoking compositions that evoke emotional and intellectual depth.

Bettina Weiß's artwork explores abstract landscapes where geometry, color and texture converge to create a universal yet deeply personal visual language. Her piece, *Portrait of a Secret Landscape*, exemplifies her mastery of form and her ability to evoke emotional and intellectual engagement through abstraction. Rendered in oil and acrylic on wood, the composition invites viewers into a dynamic interplay of time, space and color, reflecting Weiß's intuitive and constructive creative process.

Weiß's innovative use of geometric shapes forms the foundation of her work. In this piece, overlapping ovals, triangular forms and radiating lines create movement and balance. The central green triangle anchors the composition while drawing the eye outward, harmonizing contrasting elements of sharpness and softness, order and chaos.

The bold color palette, dominated by warm reds, oranges and magentas, is balanced by cooler greens and teals, creating vibrancy and harmony. A textured, weathered background contrasts with the crisp geometric forms, mirroring life's unpredictability—a recurring theme in Weiß's work.

Weiß's process is intuitive, evolving without preliminary sketches. Layers of paint build depth, with traces of earlier decisions adding authenticity. Mistakes are embraced, reflecting transformation and growth. Her work explores the relationship between microcosm and macrocosm, drawing inspiration from natural patterns and scientific models to reveal the interconnectedness of all things.

Portrait of a Secret Landscape showcases Weiß's ability to push abstraction's boundaries while maintaining emotional depth, offering viewers a transformative experience through her exploration of time, space and color.

Elise Ansel's Woman in Red II masterfully blends vibrant abstraction and historical inspiration, creating a visually stunning, transformative masterpiece.

Elise Ansel's *Woman in Red II* is a captivating abstract painting that exemplifies her transformative approach to art. Drawing inspiration from Old Master works, Ansel reimagines traditional narratives through the lens of abstraction, creating a dynamic interplay of color, texture and movement. The painting is characterized by bold, sweeping brushstrokes and a vibrant palette dominated by warm reds and pinks, contrasted with cooler tones like blue and green. These elements interact in a layered composition, evoking a sense of energy and spontaneity.

The textured brushstrokes and overlapping shapes create depth and complexity, inviting viewers to explore the painting's emotional and conceptual layers. The warm gradient background, transitioning from deep red to soft pink, provides a foundation for the dynamic interplay of colors and forms. The inclusion of contrasting hues, such as the striking blue and green strokes, adds balance and vibrancy to the composition.

Ansel's work challenges traditional artistic conventions, using abstraction to reinterpret historical themes and explore contemporary issues such as gender and inclusivity. *Woman in Red II* exemplifies her ability to deconstruct and transform classical influences into a modern, non-representational visual language. The painting's energy and luminosity reflect Ansel's mastery of color and her commitment to creating art that transcends time and place.

Through *Woman in Red II*, Ansel invites viewers into a dialogue that celebrates transformation, creativity and the enduring power of art. It is a testament to her unique ability to bridge the historical and the contemporary, offering a fresh perspective on abstraction.

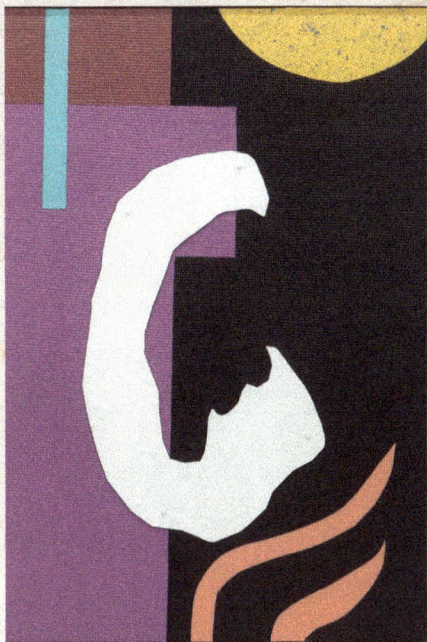

EBSTEIN CAPSULE
by Alex Ebstein

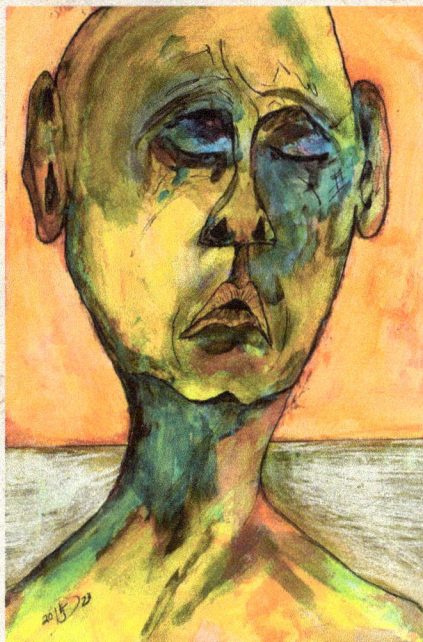

SURVIVING THE FIRE IN THE SKY
by Duane Kirby Jensen

SELF PORTRAIT
by Brandi Twilley

Alex Ebstein's visionary artistry transforms everyday materials into profound narratives, blending innovation, cultural critique, and captivating visual brilliance effortlessly.

Alex Ebstein's artwork is a masterful exploration of materiality and contemporary culture, blending tactile elements with conceptual depth. The piece, characterized by its bold geometric shapes and vibrant color palette, exemplifies her innovative use of unconventional materials such as yoga mats and gym equipment. The central white, irregular "C" shape anchors the composition, creating a dynamic interplay with the surrounding elements—a purple rectangle, a yellow semi-circle, and flame-like orange curves. These components, juxtaposed against a textured black background, evoke a sense of movement and energy, while the grid-like patterns add a tactile quality that invites closer inspection.

Ebstein's work transcends mere aesthetics, delving into themes of wellness culture, self-help, and the commodification of fitness trends. By repurposing materials associated with physical health and boutique fitness, she critiques societal obsessions with perfection and productivity. The artwork's layered textures and contrasting forms reflect the tension between the organic and the artificial, the personal and the commercial. The result is a visually striking and thought-provoking piece that challenges viewers to reconsider the objects and ideologies that permeate their daily lives.

This artwork is a testament to Ebstein's ability to merge playfulness with intellectual rigor. Her background as both an artist and curator is evident in the meticulous composition and conceptual clarity of the piece. It is a celebration of the unexpected, transforming the mundane into the extraordinary.

Alex Ebstein's work is a triumph of innovation, creativity, and cultural critique. Her ability to reimagine materials and challenge conventions is truly inspiring.

Duane Kirby Jensen's art is a profound symphony of color, emotion, and narrative, capturing the essence of human resilience and introspection.

Duane Kirby Jensen's work, *Surviving the Fire in the Sky*, is a masterful exploration of human vulnerability and resilience. The painting's evocative composition, featuring the back of a human figure gazing toward a glowing horizon, invites viewers into a deeply introspective experience. The blurred facial features of the figure create a universal quality, allowing the audience to project their own emotions onto the piece. The warm, fiery tones of the background, contrasted with cooler hues on the figure, evoke a sense of both destruction and renewal, encapsulating the duality of despair and hope.

Jensen's ability to blend abstraction with emotional realism is unparalleled. His bold brushstrokes and dynamic textures breathe life into the painting, while the surreal interplay of colors reflects his poetic sensibility. The horizon line, suggestive of a seascape or a distant landscape, anchors the composition in a tranquil yet haunting setting, emphasizing themes of isolation and contemplation. The painting's title, *Surviving the Fire in the Sky*, resonates with the environmental and existential struggles that Jensen often explores in his work, making it a poignant commentary on humanity's fragility and resilience in the face of adversity.

Drawing inspiration from Film Noir and German Expressionism, Jensen's artistry transcends traditional boundaries, merging visual and emotional depth. His unique perspective as an "outsider artist" allows him to challenge societal norms while celebrating the indomitable human spirit. This piece, like much of his oeuvre, is a testament to his ability to transform personal pain and global concerns into a universal narrative. *Surviving the Fire in the Sky* is not just a painting—it is an invitation to reflect, feel, and confront the complexities of existence.

Brandi Twilley's art masterfully transforms personal adversity into evocative, introspective works that resonate deeply with universal human experiences.

Brandi Twilley's art is a masterful blend of emotional depth, technical skill, and profound storytelling that captivates the soul. Her self-portrait is a striking exploration of identity, memory, and the human experience. The blurred face of the subject evokes a sense of mystery and introspection, inviting viewers to project their own emotions and interpretations onto the work. The dark, textured background enhances the somber mood, creating a powerful contrast with the pale skin of the subject and drawing attention to the central figure.

The minimalist composition speaks volumes through its simplicity, emphasizing the emotional weight of the piece. Twilley's use of muted tones and soft lighting creates a hauntingly beautiful atmosphere, while the deliberate obscurity of the subject's features challenges traditional notions of portraiture. This approach reflects her ability to transcend the personal and delve into universal themes of loss, resilience, and renewal.

Twilley's personal journey, marked by challenges such as house fires, depression, and physical illness, deeply informs her artistic practice. These experiences are evident in the introspective and contemplative nature of her work. The black clothing in the portrait, a recurring motif in her Crest series, symbolizes mourning and transformation, resonating with the aftermath of fire and the shared struggles of humanity.

Her ability to channel personal adversity into art that speaks to broader human experiences is a testament to her talent and vision. Brandi Twilley's self-portrait is not just a reflection of her own story but a mirror for viewers to explore their own emotions and connections to the world. It is a poignant and unforgettable piece that solidifies her place as a significant voice in contemporary art.

VULNERABILITY (2020)
by Han Yang

HOT WATER
by Alexander Deschamps

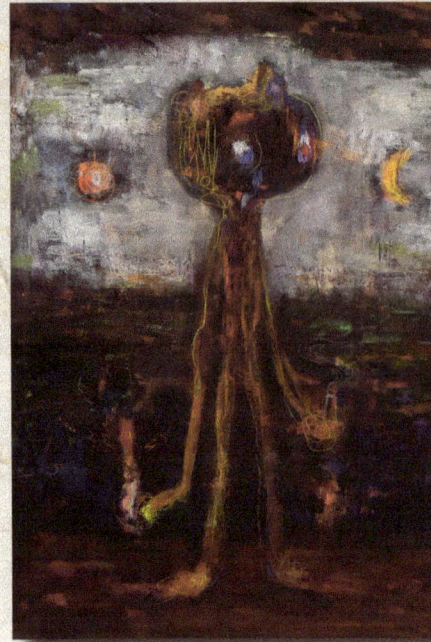

FINDING PEACE BETWEEN LİGHT AND DARK
by Wei-Ting Chen

Han Yang's 'Vulnerability' masterfully blends tradition, modernity, and symbolism, creating a visually arresting and thought-provoking masterpiece.

Alexander Deschamps masterfully blends humor, irony, and vibrant visuals, creating thought-provoking art that captivates and challenges viewers.

Wei-Ting Chen masterfully blends vivid symbolism and poetic depth, creating evocative works that resonate with emotion and universal introspection.

Han Yang's photograph, titled *Vulnerability, 2020,* is a striking visual narrative that masterfully blends minimalism with cultural and symbolic depth. Set against a bold, solid red background, the image immediately commands attention with its dramatic and intense atmosphere. The central figure, crouched low to the ground, exudes a sense of introspection and ritualistic focus. Their face is intentionally blurred, emphasizing anonymity and universality, while their long, sleek black braid extends across the floor, becoming a prominent visual element that symbolizes continuity and tradition.

The subject's exposed back, adorned with vertical black calligraphy in an East Asian script, adds a layer of cultural and narrative significance. These markings, meticulously placed, evoke themes of identity, heritage, and transformation. The attire—a black, long-sleeved garment with an open back, paired with a structured, light-colored sash reminiscent of a modernized obi—further enhances the fusion of traditional and contemporary aesthetics. The small white objects arranged in a line on the floor, possibly petals or abstract shapes, contribute an enigmatic element, inviting viewers to interpret their symbolic meaning.

Han Yang's use of color is particularly noteworthy. The deep red backdrop contrasts sharply with the black and white elements, creating a balanced yet dynamic composition. This interplay of colors, combined with the subject's deliberate posture and interaction with the objects, evokes a meditative and thought-provoking atmosphere.

The photograph exemplifies Han Yang's ability to challenge traditional narratives of femininity and identity. By merging cultural symbols with modern minimalism, she creates a visual dialogue that transcends boundaries, inviting viewers to reflect on the fluidity of identity and the interplay between tradition and progress. *Vulnerability,* is a testament to Han's artistry, blending emotion, abstraction, and cultural depth into a single, unforgettable image.

Alexander Deschamps' painting *Hot Water* is a masterful blend of humor, irony, and social commentary, encapsulating his signature style of juxtaposing playful imagery with darker undertones. The artwork features a cartoonish depiction of a blue fish and a red lobster sitting cheerfully in a cooking pot over a roaring fire. Their exaggerated smiles and animated gestures create a lighthearted and comedic atmosphere, yet the underlying irony of their oblivious predicament adds a layer of thought-provoking depth.

Deschamps' ability to balance comedy and tragedy is evident in this piece. The vibrant, saturated colors—such as the bright blue of the fish and the fiery red of the lobster—immediately draw the viewer's attention, while the dynamic flames and textured green background enhance the visual impact. The simplicity of the setting ensures that the focus remains on the central characters and their interaction, which is both amusing and unsettling. This duality is a hallmark of Deschamps' work, as he uses familiar, whimsical imagery to explore complex themes.

In *Hot Water,* the artist appears to comment on consumerism and environmental decay, themes that resonate throughout his broader body of work. The smiling sea creatures, seemingly unaware of their fate, could symbolize humanity's own ignorance or denial in the face of pressing global issues. By turning a playful scene into a subtle critique, Deschamps invites viewers to reflect on their own complicity and the absurdity of modern life.

This painting exemplifies Deschamps' unique visual language, which draws from cartoons, pop culture, and urban life to create layered narratives. It is both accessible and profound, offering an initial sense of amusement that gives way to deeper contemplation. *Hot Water* is a testament to Deschamps' ability to provoke thought and dialogue through art, making it a standout piece in his oeuvre.

Wei-Ting Chen's *Finding Peace between Light and Dark* (2023) is a poignant exploration of the delicate balance between opposing forces—light and dark, life and death, joy and sorrow. This acrylic, oil pastel, and colored pencil work on canvas (116.5 x 91 cm) is a visual and emotional journey that invites viewers to reflect on the complexities of existence. The painting is accompanied by a poetic fragment that deepens its introspective tone, hinting at the artist's ongoing search for meaning and understanding in life's transient moments.

Chen's work is deeply rooted in personal symbolism, drawing from his childhood memories and existential musings. The painting's abstract and surreal composition reflects his signature style, where intuitive graffiti-like strokes and symbolic figures create a dreamlike narrative. The interplay of vibrant and muted colors mirrors the tension between light and dark, evoking a sense of both conflict and harmony. The textured layers of the canvas suggest depth, as if the painting itself is a palimpsest of emotions and memories.

The accompanying poem, with lines like "In the gray below the rainbow" and "He knows death is about forgetting;" encapsulates the artist's reflective approach to themes of mortality and the human condition. Chen's statement, "If personal experience can reflect itself, I think drawing and writing are a kind of slice of self," resonates strongly in this piece, as it seamlessly blends visual and literary art to create a holistic narrative.

Chen's ability to weave childhood symbols—such as teddy bears and costume characters—into existential themes is a hallmark of his work. *Finding Peace between Light and Dark* is not just a painting; it is a meditative experience that invites viewers to confront their own dualities and seek their own "exit" in the gray spaces of life. This piece exemplifies Chen's mastery in creating art that is both deeply personal and universally resonant.

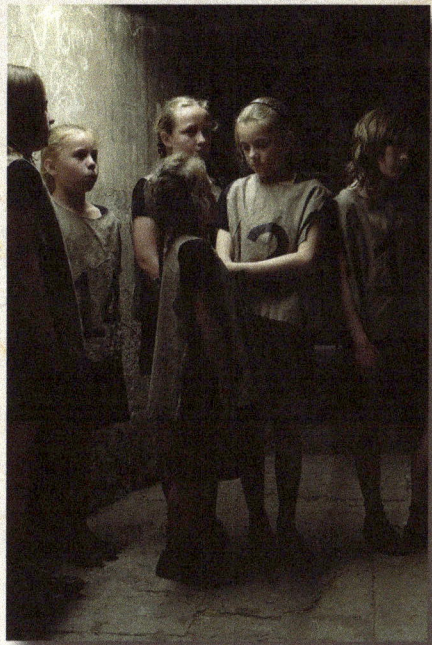

GRAND ORGAN
by Danica Dakic

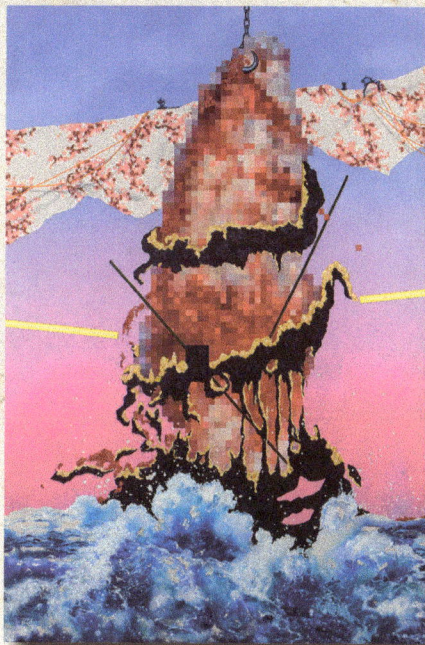

BLANKET
by Eleen Lin

PILGRIM
by Rimma Gerlovina and Valeriy Gerlovin

Dakić's Grand Organ masterfully intertwines identity, collectivity, and displacement, evoking profound emotions through its hauntingly evocative imagery.

Eleen Lin's 'Blanket' masterfully blends tradition and modernity, evoking transformation, cultural hybridity, and the fluidity of identity.

Brandi Twilley's art masterfully transforms personal adversity into evocative, introspective works that resonate deeply with universal human experiences.

Danica Dakić's *Grand Organ* is a profound visual and auditory exploration of identity, collectivity, and the interplay between justice and performance. The image accompanying this work captures a hauntingly evocative scene: a group of children, their faces blurred, gathered in a dimly lit, underground space. Dressed in uniform beige tunics marked with numbers, the children's anonymity and the stark setting evoke themes of displacement, control, and the loss of individuality within larger societal structures.

The muted tones and rough textures of the environment—cracked concrete walls, uneven stone floors, and a shadowy staircase—create a foreboding atmosphere. The children's body language, a mix of stillness and subtle interaction, suggests a quiet tension, as if they are caught between innocence and the weight of an unseen narrative. The numbers on their tunics hint at classification or dehumanization, leaving the viewer to ponder their significance.

Dakić's ability to blur the boundaries between reality and allegory is evident here. The image resonates with her broader artistic themes, such as the disconnection between personal experience and public narratives, as well as the tension between individuality and collectivity. The setting's claustrophobic feel and the children's obscured identities amplify the sense of displacement and ambiguity, hallmarks of Dakić's work.

This image, like much of Dakić's oeuvre, invites viewers to confront uncomfortable questions about power, identity, and the human condition. It is a testament to her mastery of visual storytelling and her commitment to exploring the complexities of our shared histories and societal structures. *Grand Organ* is not just a work of art—it is a meditation on the fragility and resilience of the human spirit in the face of disconnection and displacement.

Eleen Lin's B*lanket* is a captivating visual narrative that seamlessly blends traditional and contemporary elements, reflecting her multicultural identity and thematic exploration of cultural hybridity. The artwork portrays a surreal maritime scene, where a ship-like structure appears pixelated and fragmented, set against a vibrant, dreamlike backdrop. The dynamic interplay of turbulent waves, fiery tendrils, and translucent, vein-like sails creates a sense of movement and transformation.

Lin's signature technique—layering oil over acrylic—imbues the piece with depth and complexity. The acrylic base evokes the fluidity of traditional Chinese ink painting, while the oil overlay disrupts this harmony, adding texture and tension. This duality mirrors Lin's exploration of identity as fluid and multifaceted, shaped by her experiences as a "third culture kid."

The chaotic yet harmonious composition aligns with Lin's broader artistic themes, particularly her *Mythopoeia* series, which reinterprets Herman Melville's *Moby-Dick*. In *Blanket*, the fragmented and glitch-like elements suggest a narrative of disintegration and reinterpretation, echoing Lin's interest in translation and the blending of Eastern and Western mythologies. The turbulent waves and suspended sails evoke a sense of isolation and transformation, resonating with the immigrant experience and the search for belonging.

Blanket invites viewers to reflect on the dissolution of cultural boundaries and the creation of shared identities. The vibrant colors, intricate patterns, and surreal atmosphere evoke awe and introspection, making the piece both deeply personal and universally resonant. Lin's ability to weave historical narratives with contemporary imagery results in a work that challenges perceptions of adaptation and belonging, offering a profound meditation on the complexities of modern identity.

The image of Rimma Gerlovina and Valeriy Gerlovin, titled *Pilgrim 2000*, is a striking visual composition that encapsulates the duo's signature blend of conceptual depth and symbolic resonance. Known for their exploration of paradoxes and the interplay between the universal and the individual, this artwork continues their tradition of merging the philosophical with the intimate.

The image features a surreal figure whose long, textured hair dominates the frame, intertwined with thorny rose stems and vibrant red roses. The blurred face of the figure adds an enigmatic quality, inviting viewers to project their interpretations onto the piece. The juxtaposition of the soft, flowing hair with the sharp, angular thorns creates a tension between beauty and discomfort, a recurring theme in the Gerlovins' work. The vibrant red roses, symbols of fragility and passion, contrast with the stark black background, heightening the drama and isolating the subject in a timeless, otherworldly space.

This composition reflects the Gerlovins' philosophical approach to art, where visual elements serve as metaphors for the human condition. The thorns and roses evoke the duality of existence—pain and beauty, struggle and transcendence—while the blurred identity of the figure underscores the universal nature of these experiences. The image resonates with the Gerlovins' broader body of work, which often challenges viewers to question boundaries between essence and form, subject and observer.

In *Pilgrim 2000*, the Gerlovins once again demonstrate their ability to weave complex ideas into visually arresting art. The piece invites contemplation, offering a poetic meditation on the paradoxes of life and the mysteries of existence. It is a testament to their enduring legacy as artists who transcend cultural and temporal boundaries, leaving a profound impact on the contemporary art landscape.

Exploring Migration, Belonging And Justice Through Multimedia Creations

> **"**
> The layering in my work reflects the complex interplay of traditions, languages, and experiences from moving across cultures."

CECILE CHONG

Art & Culture

Cecile Chong Weaves Cultural Identity And Universal Themes In Her Multilayered Art

Cecile Chong's work blends her multicultural upbringing with universal themes of identity and belonging. Through diverse materials and mediums, her art creates dialogues around migration, history, and our interconnected humanity.

In the vibrant world of contemporary art, few voices resonate as powerfully as that of Sienna Martz. An internationally recognized sculptor and fiber artist, Sienna has carved a unique niche by intertwining traditional textile techniques with innovative material manipulation. Her commitment to sustainability shines through in every piece, as she artfully transforms plant-based, recycled, and upcycled materials into stunning works that challenge the norms of consumerism and the excesses of modern life. Each sculpture is not merely an object of beauty; it is a statement, a call to action, and a reflection of her deep-rooted ecological conscience.

Sienna's work has graced galleries and museums across the globe, from the bustling streets of New York City to the historic avenues of Rome. Her ability to engage with diverse audiences speaks to the universal themes of nature and sustainability that permeate her art. By merging aesthetic beauty with a gentle form of activism, she invites viewers to reconsider their relationship with the environment and the impact of their choices. As she continues to push the boundaries of her medium, Sienna Martz stands as a beacon of inspiration, reminding us that art can be both beautiful and transformative. In this exclusive interview with Mosaci Digest Magazine, we delve into the mind of this remarkable artist, exploring her creative process, her commitment to sustainability, and the profound messages woven into her work.

Sustainability is a key element in your work. How do you go about sourcing eco-friendly and upcycled materials for your sculptures, and how does this impact your creative process?

As an eco-conscious artist, sourcing materials is a dedicated practice in a world

Cecile Chong's artwork masterfully blends intricate figures, foliage, and fluid watercolor backgrounds, creating a serene and nostalgic atmosphere. The delicate blue monochromatic illustrations of children and a woman evoke innocence and curiosity, harmonized with dreamy, textured washes of cream and blue hues. Overhanging leafy motifs frame the composition, enhancing its connection to nature. This piece balances timeless craftsmanship with an imaginative narrative, inviting the viewer into a tranquil, evocative moment that sparks feelings of wonder and reflection.

Cecile Chong's evocative artistry masterfully bridges cultural narratives, evoking humanity's shared essence with innovation, depth, and profound storytelling.

where most readily available supplies are often unsustainable. Depending on the art piece, I love sourcing secondhand clothing and fabrics at local thrift stores. Beyond that, I scour the internet searching for the most sustainable alternatives to common materials like organic kapok fiber instead of polyester stuffing, organic cotton instead of conventional cotton, and bamboo felt instead of wool felt. The plant fibers I choose to work with are incredibly high-quality which elevates my work. When working with secondhand fabrics, often the variety of woven textures and color palettes that come together while I source these supplies will help dictate how the artwork comes to life.

Your sculptures explore the adaptability of nature while critiquing unsustainable practices, especially in the textile industry. How do you balance aesthetic beauty with activism in your pieces?

I like to describe my work as a gentle form of activism. The artist in me has a primal desire to create beautiful works of art relating to nature that are both inviting and inspiring. And the activist in me has the desire to use my artistic voice as a means to encourage a more sustainable and ethical world.

Your work has been exhibited globally, from Berlin to Seoul. How do you think your sculptures resonate with audiences across different cultures, particularly in relation to environmental consciousness?

My hope is that viewers will reimagine

the role of art in society, positioning my work not just as an object of beauty but as a catalyst for cultural transformation and sustainable thinking. However, since my artwork does not always visually convey concerns about climate change, animal welfare, and overconsumption viewers may not always make these connections. But because my work mimics organic and abstract forms, my work inevitably provokes thought and a kinship with the natural world regardless of the audience because we, as humans, have an innate curiosity when it comes to the natural world.

You employ both traditional textile techniques and alternative material manipulation in your sculptures. Can you describe how you merge these techniques, and what drew you to explore fiber as your primary medium?

My training in fiber arts was generally rooted in contemporary, alternative exploration rather than traditional approaches. While I learned techniques such as machine sewing and fabric dying, my mentors encouraged me to think outside of tradition and develop my own techniques of sculpting with fibers. I've always been drawn to the softness of fibers and its forgiving nature. This medium has allowed me to explore my fascination with nature through an abstract and vibrant lens.

As an artist dedicated to challenging consumerism and excess, how do you navigate the commercial art world while staying true to your ecological

principles?

As an artist emerging within a digital culture, I've found utilizing commercial art forms such as social media has tremendously helped me grow my profession. I've spent years establishing my Instagram account and as a result, I have a devoted community of fellow artists and collectors who can follow and support my artistic journey. This platform has allowed me to share my ecological principles and bring more awareness to issues such as climate change, the textile waste crisis, and so on.

Your works are often described as inspired by the geometry of biology. Can you elaborate on how the natural world informs the textures, shapes, and colors in your art?

I have a deep fascination with how cells and organisms are formed through patterns and replication. I often use the transformative power of replication of a single form to create my sculptural pieces – building, layering, and structuring my work into something unexpected and quite fascinating.

Ivy Zhang

Ivy Zhang, the visionary Brand Director of Ulofey.com, is a shining example of what passion, dedication, and a pursuit of excellence can achieve in a highly specialised industry. As part of a family deeply embedded in the wig sector for over three decades, Ivy has turned heritage into innovation, transforming Ulofey into a trusted name synonymous with quality and authenticity. Her unwavering commitment to crafting exceptional products—combined with a profound understanding of customer needs—has elevated the brand to global recognition while retaining its deeply personal and human touch.

Under Ivy's leadership, Ulofey has become a beacon of empowerment, particularly for women navigating hair loss. Her focus on pioneering advancements such as breathable wig caps and streamlined production processes reflects both ingenuity and a heartfelt dedication to improving lives. Beyond their exquisite craftsmanship, Ulofey has cultivated a sense of community, offering not just products but also unwavering support to those in need. Ivy's vision, rooted in ethical sourcing, bespoke service, and an unrelenting pursuit of excellence, is nothing short of inspiring—a true testament to the legacy and future of this extraordinary family-owned brand. We are thrilled to spotlight Ivy Zhang's groundbreaking work and insights in this issue of *Beauty Prime*.

Ivy Zhang *discusses Ulofey's commitment to ethically sourced materials, groundbreaking designs, bespoke craftsmanship, and creating an empowering community for those experiencing hair loss.*

Ulofey Transforms The Wig Industry With Quality, Craftsmanship And Empowerment

Innovation And Compassion Redefining The Wig Experience

Ulofey emphasizes direct sourcing of virgin and Remy human hair—can you walk us through how this impacts both product quality and pricing for your customers?

Our extensive industry experience allows us to directly source raw materials, completely bypassing intermediary markups. This ensures we acquire the highest quality human hair while maintaining competitive pricing for our customers. It's a direct benefit of our integrated approach to sourcing and production.

Your new breathable wig cap design sounds groundbreaking—what kind of feedback have you received so far from customers in Europe or those with medical hair loss?

Our dedicated team of highly skilled artisans creates bespoke products tailored to individual customer needs, and our breathable wig cap design is a key innovation. We're proud to report that we've experienced no returns for custom cap orders, with customers consistently expressing satisfaction. This positive feedback often translates into strong repeat business from our loyal users.

With a typical custom wig turnaround of just 10 business days, how does Ulofey

manage to balance speed with the high level of hand craftsmanship involved?

Our ability to offer a swift 10-business-day turnaround for custom wigs is a direct result of our integrated production process. By utilizing our own skilled artisans in-house, we eliminate the need for third-party processing. This streamlined approach allows us to maintain our high standards of hand craftsmanship while ensuring timely delivery, all driven by our commitment to customer satisfaction.

How does Ulofey's collaboration with local salons and virtual consultations enhance the customization experience for clients?

Currently, we do not have formal collaborations with local salons, though we do have plans to explore such partnerships in the future. Our primary focus remains on direct virtual consultations, which allow us to thoroughly understand each client's preferences. While we acknowledge the limitations of online interactions, such as the inability to physically feel the product or perfectly gauge color, we are actively planning future salon experience stores and pop-up events. These initiatives will provide direct, tangible engagement with our consumers, enhancing the overall customization journey.

As a family-owned business that has grown into a global brand, what core values have remained constant since Ulofey's beginnings?

Since Ulofey's inception, our core values have consistently revolved around two fundamental principles: quality as our foremost priority and a steadfast commitment to meeting every customer's individual needs with personalized solutions. These values guide every decision we make, from sourcing raw materials to crafting our final products.

Ulofey has built a community around hair loss support—can you share more about this initiative and how it contributes to your broader mission of empowerment?

Our hair loss support community is primarily focused on empowering women experiencing hair loss by fostering confidence and providing a sense of belonging. This initiative aims to create a supportive space where individuals can find encouragement, share experiences, and ultimately feel more confident in their journey. It directly contributes to Ulofey's broader mission of empowerment, extending beyond just providing products to building a supportive network.

Art & Culture

Matt Gondek's visionary Deconstructive Pop Art boldly disrupts iconic imagery, combining playfulness with a punk spirit to redefine pop culture's symbols.

His art merges vibrant colors with deconstructed icons, embodying rebellion and critique. In this interview, he discusses punk roots, art business challenges balancing approachability with dark themes of anarchy and pessimism.

Matt Gondek, an innovator in Deconstructive Pop Art, has established himself as a defining voice in contemporary art, reshaping the way we interpret icons of pop culture. Known for his audacious style and unapologetic dismantling of familiar cartoon heroes, Gondek's work pairs a vivid, punchy color palette with a punk ethos that celebrates rebellion and critiques the allure of mainstream idols. His art, a fusion of high-energy destruction and nostalgia, is both a tribute and a deconstruction of modern mythologies, challenging viewers to reconsider the value we place on cultural icons. Gondek's pieces have captivated audiences worldwide, leading to sold-out exhibitions in cultural hubs like Los Angeles, New York, Paris beyond.

In this interview, Gondek opens up about his DIY beginnings, the inspirations drawn from childhood heroes his unapologetic approach to the art business. Gondek reveals what it means to be a self-made artist in a world of gatekeepers, explaining how he balances the practicalities of the art industry with a raw, unfiltered creative voice.

Matt Gondek on Art, Icons Anarchy

The artist reveals his DIY journey and punk rock influences

How do you define "Deconstructive Pop Art," and what elements do you believe are essential to this style in your work?

I spent a lot of time in punk bands I learned about DIY ethics. I've always leaned that way – I question authority and tear down hierarchy, so that's where the deconstruction part comes from. The icons come from my childhood heroes like Mickey Mouse and Bart Simpson. I tear down these icons through my work, so that's deconstructive pop art.

Can you share the inspiration behind your unique approach to deconstructing cartoon icons and pop culture figures?

There's been a few. Andy Warhol, who's from Pittsburgh, like me. He didn't influence me in the sense that our styles are the same, but he influenced me in terms of the networking and business side of the artwork and his business acumen.

Also Roy Lichtenstein and his Ben-Day dots were a key influence. Lichtenstein is my favourite artist I like how he took comic books and cartoons and turned them into fine art using the same printing methods – it's fascinating.

Your work features a vibrant colour palette and playful tone. How do these choices reflect your message or critique of societal norms?

I use bright and poppy colours because it makes the work more approachable and digestible. By painting things bright and fun, I'm able to reach a wider audience while still dealing with things like pessimism, addiction, anarchy, etc.

What role does your punk rock spirit play in your artistic process and the themes you explore in your work?

The biggest takeaway from punk rock is the Do-It-Yourself mentality. When I began as an artist I put on my own shows, made my own clothes and prints, etc. Now, the anti-authority and self betterment side of Punk comes through more in the work.

As a self-taught artist, what challenges have you faced in developing your voice how have you overcome them?

The higher up the ladder you go in the art world, the more doors are in your way - and it really is all about who you know.

The biggest challenge I faced starting out was that I didn't know anyone.

Through your podcast, Clean Break, you discuss the business aspects of creativity. How do you balance the commercial side of art with your artistic integrity?

I don't balance them - because I've always been of the mindset that I make artwork to sustain myself. I think most artists WANT to quit their jobs and solely support themselves off of their art, but they don't know how - or are to afraid to make the changes to do it. That's what the podcast is about - how to make those changes.

Art & Culture

Blending Eastern and Western Traditions

Eleen Lin's multicultural background inspires her paintings, merging mythology, identity, and translation to explore the fluidity of cultural boundaries, fostering dialogues that connect shared human experiences across the globe.

Eleen Lin Explores Myth, Identity, And Cultural Convergence In Contemporary Art

Eleen Lin masterfully bridges cultures and histories with evocative paintings that highlight the universal complexities of identity and belonging.

By MOSAIC DIGEST STAFF

Eleen Lin's art offers a vivid exploration of culture, mythology, and identity, showcasing the dynamic intersection of Eastern and Western traditions through her unique creative lens. Born in Taiwan, raised in Thailand, and educated in England and the U.S., Lin embodies the complexities of being a "third culture kid." Her experiences of living across cultures have profoundly shaped her artistic practice, allowing her to navigate and blend diverse narratives into poignant visual expressions.

Lin describes today's era as "the age of cultural cannibalism," where elements from varied histories and geographies intersect and morph into new identities. This notion serves as a guiding principle in her work. Beginning her artistic journey as a child, she turned to painting as a way to communicate when language barriers hindered her ability to express herself after her family moved to Thailand. Later, while studying in England, she delved into Chinese art history and ink painting—a connection to her heritage that would influence her signature technique of layering oil paint over acrylic. This method creates a duality: the acrylic evokes the fluidity of traditional Chinese ink painting, while the oil disrupts it, introducing depth and complexity. Her work constantly examines the interplay of cultural convergence and fragmentation.

In her *Pet Society* series, Lin explores the deep, often mystical connection between urban dwellers and their pets. Inspired by Chinese folklore—particularly tales of shape-shifting animal spirits and human relationships—Lin weaves these narratives into modern urbanity. After moving to New York and adopting a cat named Meme, Lin became fascinated by how urbanites form intense emotional bonds with their pets, often deeper than connections with other humans. She incorporates this dynamic into her art, reflecting on themes of identity, belonging, and modern isolation, while simultaneously offering visual commentaries on the curious intersections of culture and contemporary life.

Her more recent series, *Mythopoeia*, reimagines Herman Melville's *Moby-Dick* through the prism of Lin's own identity as an immigrant artist. Instead of focusing on the novel's familiar themes of obsession and morality, she reinterprets it with attention to its cultural diversity, isolation, and global dimensions. Lin identified resonances between the Pequod's multicultural crew and her personal journey—bringing her immigrant experience to bear on this quintessentially American text. Her fascination with translation plays a prominent role in this series. Comparing the novel's original English to various Chinese translations, Lin uncovers the mistranslations and altered nuances that arise through cultural and linguistic shifts. These mistranslations often result in unexpected meanings, and Lin uses them as opportunities to blend Eastern and Western ideologies and mythologies in her paintings. By embedding layers of reinterpretation, Lin transforms *Moby-Dick* into a work that transcends cultures, exploring themes of diaspora, memory, and identity within the context of today's globalized world.

Lin's academic background significantly shaped her artistic voice. At the Slade School of Fine Art in London, she encountered Western traditions like German Expressionism, which spurred her to reflect on her own cultural identity and rediscover her connection to Chinese art. Her time at Yale School of Art in the U.S., with its emphasis on formalism, redefined her approach to storytelling and composition. These experiences encouraged her to strike a balance between Eastern and Western aesthetics while embracing the fluidity of identity in her work.

Exhibiting internationally, Lin has connected with audiences worldwide, each offering distinct interpretations of her art. Her exploration of cultural boundaries, translation, and identity invites dialogue and introspection. Viewers often relate the symbols and narratives in her paintings to their own experiences, underscoring the universality of her themes. Lin embraces this diversity of response, seeing it as affirmation of art's ability to bridge cultural divides.

Through her remarkable career, Lin has exhibited in prominent museums and galleries across Asia, Europe, and the Americas, earning awards like the Elizabeth Canfield Hicks Award and hosting works in permanent collections such as the National Taiwan Museum of Fine Arts and the Jimenez-Colon Collection. As she continues working in New York, Lin's art remains a testament to the evolving, multidimensional nature of identity and the profound narratives that arise when cultures collide and coalesce. Her work does not simply reflect these shifts but actively reshapes

"

My work acts as a collective journal, documenting the erosion of cultural boundaries and emphasizing the interconnectedness of experiences."

Eleen Lin

A Story Of Passion, Experimentation And Spiritual Expression

Janice Taylor's art blends faith, personal revelation, and global experiences, showcasing her innovative use of mixed media and interpretive artistry inspired by her Christian journey and mission-driven collaborations worldwide.

Janice Taylor's evolution into a full-time artist mirrors the vibrancy and depth of her creations. Known for her evocative and interpretive artwork, Janice's pieces are a compelling blend of faith, personal experience, and cultural immersion. Her mixed media explorations—whether through gelli printing, charcoal, painting, or art on unconventional surfaces like tea-bag paper—are celebrated for their innovative approach. However, what truly sets her apart is the spiritual core of her artistry, driven by a profound commitment to conveying themes of faith and community.

Janice's journey began in the classroom as a high school teacher, where creativity was integral to both her teaching methods and her students' learning experiences. Later, as she transitioned to mission work, she developed training materials and curricula with the same imaginative mindset. This foundation served as a springboard for her artistic journey. "My creative processes have always been at the forefront," she reflects, adding that her subject matter often emerges from personal moments of faith or images drawn from scripture. "Sometimes, I paint from imagination or sketches I've made during travels," she shares, infusing her exploration with spontaneity and depth.

Janice's Christian faith is central to her work as an artist. She describes her art as interpretive, inviting viewers to derive their own meanings. While she has no objection to the term "prophetic art," she prefers the openness of interpretation. This philosophy underpins her practice, particularly when painting live at church services and conferences. "I have no idea at the start what I'll paint or what colors to use—it's a total reliance on God's Spirit," she explains. Her faith has been her primary motivator, anchoring her transition from her headship role in learning and development to full-time artistry.

A hallmark of Janice's style is her willingness to experiment with different mediums and techniques, driven by an innate curiosity. "Art is about having fun," Janice remarks, revealing her process of entering the studio without a clear plan and allowing inspiration to strike. Whether it's experimenting with materials like teabag paper or embracing trending techniques, she views even the missteps as valuable learning experiences. This playful experimentation speaks to the joy and curiosity evident in her work.

Her extensive travels and experiences with international teams have also left an indelible mark on her artistic identity. During her time with Operation Mobilisation's Inspiro Arts Alliance, Janice collaborated with artists across disciplines, from musicians to actors. Challenges, like adapting to mixed media for the first time in Belgium or working alongside seasoned artists in Italy, shaped her confidence and technique. These early forays into public art have since evolved into a hallmark of her practice, enriching her creative output and global perspective.

Transitioning to a full-time art career wasn't without its hurdles. Leaving her structured role in learning and development for the unpredictability of arts ministry required faith and determination. Financial challenges emerged, as did the need to forge partnerships with fellow Christian artists. However, Janice's proactive and motivated nature enabled her to create opportunities both locally and abroad. She recalls poignant moments of connection, such as painting faith-filled images on her windows during lockdown, which resonated with her community. "Children would ask their parents to slow the car to look at the paintings," she recalls, a testimony to how her art became a tool for engagement and compassion.

Even in retirement, Janice continues to inspire. From canal boat outreaches to ongoing invitations for art ministry, her work remains a dynamic blend of faith, creativity, and service. Janice sums it up best: "I guess I'm not retired but re-ty-red," she says with a smile—a fitting metaphor for an artist who has built her life around renewal and reinvention.

Janice Taylor Redefines Faith and Creativity Through Her Unique Artistic Journey

Art & Culture

Janice Taylor masterfully combines creativity and faith, captivating audiences with her imaginative artistry and heartfelt dedication to meaningful storytelling.

" *My creative processes have always been at the forefront in whatever I was involved in."*

Janice Taylor

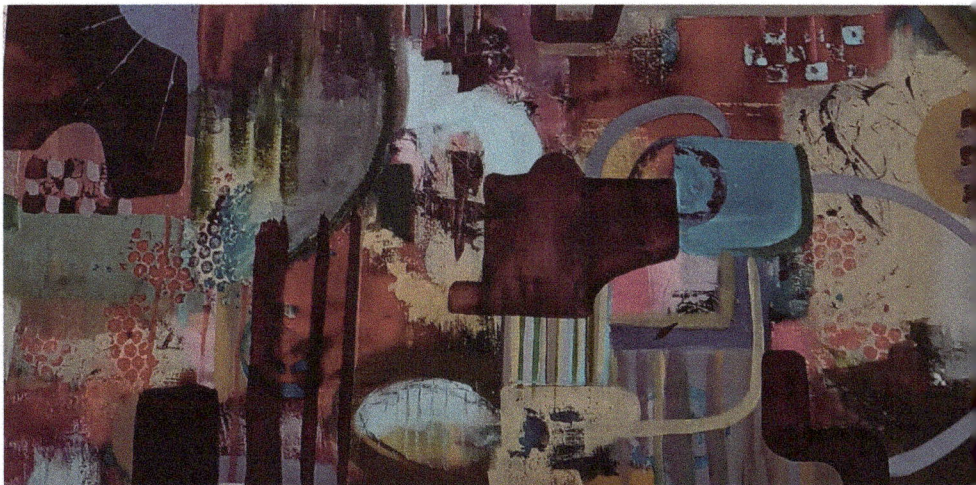

Photo by Soapbox Arts

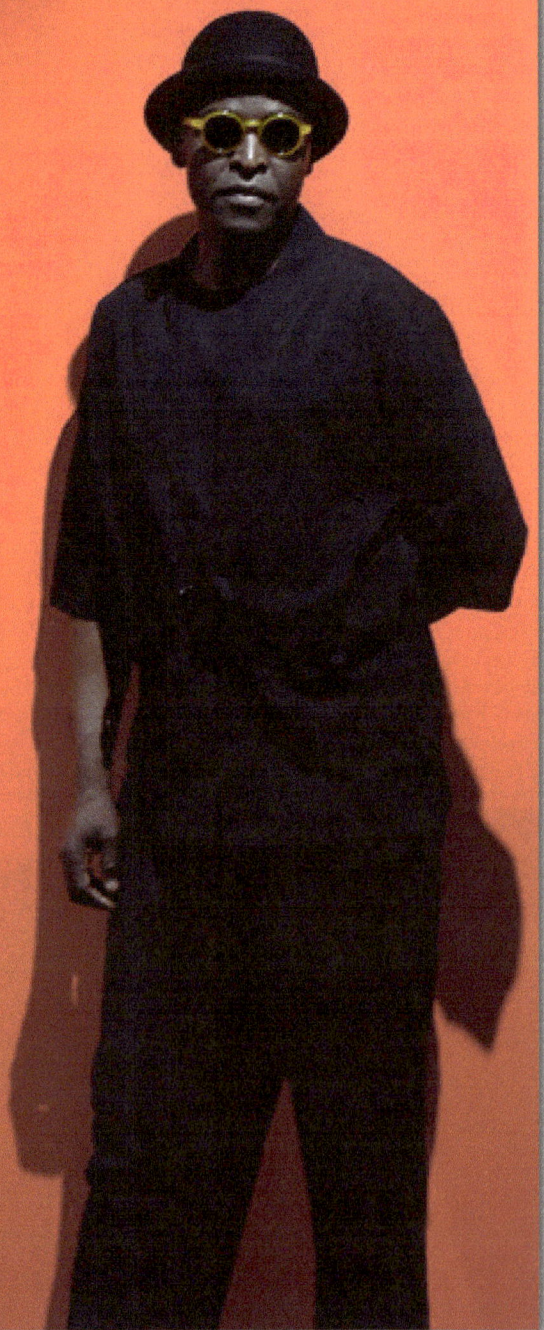

Art & Culture

Januario Jano Exploring Identity And Home In A Globalized World

Art As A Platform For Cultural Dialogue And Social Transformation

Januario Jano's interdisciplinary art explores identity, cultural narratives, and globalization. Integrating research and diverse mediums, he creates transformative pieces, fostering cultural innovation and community dialogue through artistic and social initiatives.

Januario Jano is a name that resonates deeply in the contemporary art world—a multifaceted artist whose work transcends mediums and boundaries. From sculpture and video to photography, textile, sound installation, and performance, Jano's practice is a tapestry of cultural commentary, personal introspection, and social critique. With a Master's Degree in Fine Arts from Goldsmiths University in London, his work is steeped in research, allowing him to confront poignant themes like identity, home, and cultural narratives with depth and nuance. Speaking with MOsaic Digest, Jano opened up about his process, inspirations, and philosophies, offering a glimpse into the mind of an artist who not only creates but also catalyzes cultural and social transformation. Through both his art and his community initiatives, such as the Angola-based cultural collective Pés Descalços and the launch of TEDxLuanda, Jano is solidifying his position as a global artistic force, bridging past and present, fiction and reality.

The Intersection of Mediums: Building Bridges Through Art

Jano's art is a constellation of mediums, each one selected with precision to serve and enhance the ideas he seeks to communicate. His approach begins with rigorous research, a process he describes as both grounding and open to surprise. "The research phase offers both a grounding foundation and a sense of openness to unexpected shifts," he shared. "It can serve as a point of departure, facilitate and clarify the core themes or ideas I want to explore, but at the same time, it leaves room for those ideas to evolve or take new forms as I engage with the materials." By embracing a range of mediums—from tactile forms like sculpture and textile to the fluid temporality of video and sound installations—Jano creates an interplay that enriches his overall practice. "The interplay between these mediums enhances the overall depth of the work, as each medium can push the boundaries of how I communicate an idea," he explained.

Fiction, Reality, and the Stories We Tell Ourselves

At the heart of Jano's work lies a constant negotiation between fiction and reality, particularly in the context of identity and cultural narratives. For the artist, this dynamic provides both a window into contemporary issues and a framework to question deeper societal constructs. "The balance between fiction and reality in my work speaks to the complex layers of identity and cultural narratives," Jano said. "These topics challenge perceptions of what is 'true' or 'authentic' in the stories we tell or hear about ourselves and our cultures." This duality is an essential lens through which Jano approaches themes like migration, globalization, and the representation of marginalized communities. Fiction, he argues, provides a valuable space for reimagining or reframing reality, helping to address power dynamics, historic narratives, and the interconnected factors molding the global social fabric.

Art as a Response to Globalization: Collaboration and Critique

Globalization—both its opportunities and its pitfalls—is a recurring theme in Jano's art. He views the phenomenon as a crucial lens for examining the interplay of cultures, economies, and technologies, as well as a mechanism for interrogating identity. "In an increasingly interconnected world, the blending of cultures, economies, and technologies creates new spaces for dialogue but also raises questions of power, ownership, and identity," he reflected. Through his work, Jano creates spaces where histories and narratives collide, allowing abstract ideas—like the cultural flows brought on by globalization—to gain tangible, physical form. This critique of globalization is not merely an artistic exercise but a call for reflection. "Art becomes a platform to reflect on how globalization reshapes our understanding of self and other, exposing the ways identities are constructed, deconstructed, and recontextualized in this global context," he explained.

This striking installation from Januario Jano's solo exhibition, Butaiuri in Tokyo 2024, masterfully juxtaposes texture, color, and form. The central sphere showcases intricate beadwork, drawing the viewer's eye with a vivid mosaic of black, white, red, and blue. The hanging textile contrasts with its rugged, fragmented appearance, blending glossy black, fiery orange, and coarse materials. Set against a bold red backdrop, the dramatic and minimalistic setting intensifies the artwork's emotional resonance. Jano skillfully explores themes of imperfection, cultural identity, and materiality, creating a visually captivating and thought-provoking piece.

Cultural Leadership and the Role of the Artist

Beyond his own practice, Jano is deeply invested in cultural development and social transformation. His initiatives, such as Pés Descalços and TEDxLuanda, exemplify his belief that art and cultural innovation should have a broad, tangible impact on communities. "Pés Descalços started as I felt the need to engage and contribute to the local cultural and artistic landscape outside my own practice," Jano said. "These cultural initiatives are parallel to my artistic practice in fostering community, dialogue, and engagement with cultural narratives." Rather than viewing his artistic practice and community initiatives as separate entities, Jano integrates them, embodying a philosophy that art should have both personal and public resonance. "I see the artist as both a creator and a facilitator, someone who bridges diverse perspectives, encouraging collective reflection, social development, and critical thinking," he affirmed.

Decoding Identity Through Research and the Material World

Jano's art is deeply informed by research—a key element that underpins every step of his creative process. His studious approach allows him to excavate layers of meaning,

uncovering connections between themes like identity, home, and cultural memory. "When dealing with themes like identity and home, the research might involve delving into historical narratives, personal stories, cultural identity, and production," Jano explained. The resulting work is a harmony of the conceptual and the material, with mediums chosen to amplify the project's core themes. For instance, Jano might explore the concept of "home" through the architectural, emotional, and cultural dimensions of space, while a study of identity might draw on post-colonial theory, displacement, or oral histories. "These multidisciplinary approaches offer a rich context that informs the final decisions of the project in hand," he said.

The Body as a Canvas of Culture and History

The body is a recurring symbol within Jano's practice, representing the nexus of space, culture, and history. As both a physical and metaphorical vessel, the body becomes a site where these complex themes come alive. "The body in my work plays a pivotal role— it acts as a symbol, representing the intersection of space, culture, and history," Jano shared. His projects explore how the body carries both memory and meaning, functioning as a site of negotiation and contestation

within broader societal frameworks. Jano's depiction of the body varies across projects. In some cases, it appears through physicality, as in his sculptures or performances, while in others, its absence or fragmentation is evoked through video, photography, or sound installations. The flexibility in these representations underscores Jano's ability to adapt his artistic language to match the nuances of each project's message.

Looking Forward: A Path of Connection and Transformation

Januario Jano is redefining what it means to be an artist in a globalized world. His ability to weave research, storytelling, and a diverse range of materials into a cohesive artistic vision transforms his work into more than just a visual experience—it becomes a powerful commentary on identity, cultural evolution, and the forces shaping our shared future. Through his artistic practice and his roles as a cultural leader, Jano has made it clear that art is not just about aesthetics but also about building bridges, challenging norms, and fostering transformation. As he continues to innovate and explore, his work serves as a compelling reminder of art's potential to illuminate the complexities of the human condition in an ever-connected world.

Source: WOWWART

Shaping Beauty Through Authentic Materials

"

Art never lies, it only reveals."

DIANE PIERI

Diane Pieri Inspires With Her Timeless Vision And Dedication To Artistic Excellence

Diane Pieri shares her artistic journey, exploring authenticity, emotional expression, cultural influences like Indian miniatures, and her unyielding commitment to innovation, invention, and the pursuit of beauty in her work.

Diane Pieri's extraordinary artistic journey stands as a testament to creativity, perseverance, and the boundless exploration of beauty. With an illustrious career spanning over five decades, Pieri has established herself as a visionary force in the art world, merging cultural traditions, symbolic meanings, and contemporary innovations into a body of work that captivates the soul and ignites the imagination. Her mastery of delicate techniques, her fearless use of authentic materials like 23-carat gold leaf and handmade papers, and her profound ability to draw inspiration from diverse sources, such as Indian miniatures and folk art, define an artist who is unafraid to push artistic boundaries while remaining deeply rooted in truth and authenticity.

Pieri's work is more than visual art—it is an invitation into worlds of radiant color, intricate patterns, and emotional depth. Whether crafting enormous public sculptures, murals that speak to communities, or intimate pieces that reveal the inner workings of her heart and mind, Pieri imbues each creation with a sense of wonder and meaning. Her art exists at the intersection of craftsmanship and emotion, offering a glimpse into her continual pursuit of invention and beauty, as well as her unwavering devotion to sharing joy with others.

In this exclusive interview, Diane Pieri reflects on her inspirations, motivations, and the inner drive that has fueled her incredible body of work. From her early fascination with art as a young child to her profound respect for cultural storytelling and innovative techniques, Pieri shares insights into her creative process, her challenges, and her ability to continually evolve. Prepare to be inspired by her wisdom, passion, and unrelenting com-

EDITOR'S NOTE: Diane Pieri's work is a vibrant, dynamic exploration of color, pattern, and form, embodying her signature fusion of cultural influences and contemporary innovation. The accordion-style folding artwork dazzles with bold hues—magenta, yellow, purple—and intricate motifs reminiscent of Indian miniatures and folk art, reflecting her decades-long reverence for cross-cultural storytelling. The piece's rhythmic circles and organic shapes evoke joy and movement, while its layered structure invites interaction, mirroring Pieri's belief in art as an immersive experience. Her use of authentic materials and meticulous craftsmanship shines through, reinforcing her commitment to beauty and authenticity. This work is a testament to her fearless creativity, blending tradition with playful experimentation to create a visual symphony that resonates with emotional depth and exuberance.

mitment to offering beauty in the everyday.

How do you balance the use of symbolic meaning and abstract patterns in your work, and what role does each play in conveying your artistic message?

Every artist, over time, develops a language. What I aspire to do is have and use a language that I don't think about, like using English. I don't think about talking or formulating a sentence but, there are various times when I do search for a specific word to use, a more complex descriptive word. This is how it is making art.

Authenticity is a core principle in your art. How do the materials you choose, like 23 carat gold leaf and handmade papers, enhance the meaning of your work?

It is of utmost importance to me, as a human being, that I am authentic, in my relationships, in my word, in my actions, in my art. Art never lies, it only reveal. My art reveals who I am. This happens with everyone whether they are an artist or not. Of course children reveal all the time and are then taught to lie. I must use authentic materials because they help imbue my art with beauty, cultural integrity, sincerity, courage and strength.

Indian miniatures have deeply influenced your artistic journey. How do these influences manifest in your creations, both visually and conceptually?

I have been influenced by Indian miniatures for over 30 years now. They originally captured me because of their delicacy, their

different cultural expression, their color, design and story telling. A whole world of possibilities opened up to me when I seriously started to study Indian miniatures. In fact, when I first applied for a grant to go to India, I studied with a young Indian painter so I could learn technique- how to paint a bush, a tree, grass, flowers, cloth. That first trip was thwarted by 9/11. I applied for another grant in 2012 and finally went to Northern India. What I found was completely unexpected! This was good! I discovered Indian Folk Art, which liberated me into realms of joy, dance, uncalculated vibrancy and new visual experiences. Now I have combined all the variations of this rich language- the decreet miniatures and the playful folk art.

The quote in your studio speaks to burning passion, enthusiasm, and perseverance. How do these qualities shape your creative process and the challenges you face as an artist?

I always knew I wanted to be an artist, from the age of 6 when my crayon drawing was chosen to hang in the principal's office. My parents were always very supportive throughout my educational years. However, this does not mean that I have not cried bitter tears and packed up my studio a couple of times over my long art life. As I used to tell my college students- Being an artist is a hard life, but it is a great life. I also told them that if they couldn't take rejection, they should get out then, right then.

In your pursuit to offer beauty in the everyday, what role does emotional expression play in the patterns and symbols you incorporate into your art?

Invention and beauty are what I am after. At this point in my long career, I do not differentiate between thinking and doing. This gets me into trouble. I know I am an emotional person, a feeling person, a focused person with an innate and educated understanding of color, design and all of the formal art elements. Beginning artists have a mental checklist of the formal elements and use this list to see if they have included them in their work. I do not do this anymore. For me, the important key is to kick everyone out of the studio, including myself, to paraphrase John Cage. Only then do I wander around in the space that most understands me, in search of beauty and invention.

After 25 years of artistic practice, how do you see your work evolving in the future, and what continues to inspire your exploration of new techniques or materials?

I live in fear of repeating myself! I hope I never hear anyone say that they thought they had seen the "new" work in a previous exhibition. I go on what I call "scrounging missions", after I have completed a series. This is a painful, emptiness until something unpredicted sparks my imagination. It takes patience and fortitude until something breaks through.

Source: WOWWART

Exploring Migration, Belonging And Justice Through Multimedia Creations

> "The layering in my work reflects the complex interplay of traditions, languages, and experiences from moving across cultures."

CECILE CHONG

Cecile Chong Weaves Cultural Identity And Universal Themes In Her Multilayered Art

Cecile Chong's work blends her multicultural upbringing with universal themes of identity and belonging. Through diverse materials and mediums, her art creates dialogues around migration, history, and our interconnected humanity.

In the vibrant world of contemporary art, few voices resonate as powerfully as that of Sienna Martz. An internationally recognized sculptor and fiber artist, Sienna has carved a unique niche by intertwining traditional textile techniques with innovative material manipulation. Her commitment to sustainability shines through in every piece, as she artfully transforms plant-based, recycled, and upcycled materials into stunning works that challenge the norms of consumerism and the excesses of modern life. Each sculpture is not merely an object of beauty; it is a statement, a call to action, and a reflection of her deep-rooted ecological conscience.

Sienna's work has graced galleries and museums across the globe, from the bustling streets of New York City to the historic avenues of Rome. Her ability to engage with diverse audiences speaks to the universal themes of nature and sustainability that permeate her art. By merging aesthetic beauty with a gentle form of activism, she invites viewers to reconsider their relationship with the environment and the impact of their choices. As she continues to push the boundaries of her medium, Sienna Martz stands as a beacon of inspiration, reminding us that art can be both beautiful and transformative. In this exclusive interview with Mosaci Digest Magazine, we delve into the mind of this remarkable artist, exploring her creative process, her commitment to sustainability, and the profound messages woven into her work.

Sustainability is a key element in your work. How do you go about sourcing eco-friendly and upcycled materials for your sculptures, and how does this impact your creative process?

As an eco-conscious artist, sourcing materials is a dedicated practice in a world

Cecile Chong's artwork masterfully blends intricate figures, foliage, and fluid watercolor backgrounds, creating a serene and nostalgic atmosphere. The delicate blue monochromatic illustrations of children and a woman evoke innocence and curiosity, harmonized with dreamy, textured washes of cream and blue hues. Overhanging leafy motifs frame the composition, enhancing its connection to nature. This piece balances timeless craftsmanship with an imaginative narrative, inviting the viewer into a tranquil, evocative moment that sparks feelings of wonder and reflection.

Cecile Chong's evocative artistry masterfully bridges cultural narratives, evoking humanity's shared essence with innovation, depth, and profound storytelling.

where most readily available supplies are often unsustainable. Depending on the art piece, I love sourcing secondhand clothing and fabrics at local thrift stores. Beyond that, I scour the internet searching for the most sustainable alternatives to common materials like organic kapok fiber instead of polyester stuffing, organic cotton instead of conventional cotton, and bamboo felt instead of wool felt. The plant fibers I choose to work with are incredibly high-quality which elevates my work. When working with secondhand fabrics, often the variety of woven textures and color palettes that come together while I source these supplies will help dictate how the artwork comes to life.

Your sculptures explore the adaptability of nature while critiquing unsustainable practices, especially in the textile industry. How do you balance aesthetic beauty with activism in your pieces?

I like to describe my work as a gentle form of activism. The artist in me has a primal desire to create beautiful works of art relating to nature that are both inviting and inspiring. And the activist in me has the desire to use my artistic voice as a means to encourage a more sustainable and ethical world.

Your work has been exhibited globally, from Berlin to Seoul. How do you think your sculptures resonate with audiences across different cultures, particularly in relation to environmental consciousness?

My hope is that viewers will reimagine

the role of art in society, positioning my work not just as an object of beauty but as a catalyst for cultural transformation and sustainable thinking. However, since my artwork does not always visually convey concerns about climate change, animal welfare, and overconsumption viewers may not always make these connections. But because my work mimics organic and abstract forms, my work inevitably provokes thought and a kinship with the natural world regardless of the audience because we, as humans, have an innate curiosity when it comes to the natural world.

You employ both traditional textile techniques and alternative material manipulation in your sculptures. Can you describe how you merge these techniques, and what drew you to explore fiber as your primary medium?

My training in fiber arts was generally rooted in contemporary, alternative exploration rather than traditional approaches. While I learned techniques such as machine sewing and fabric dying, my mentors encouraged me to think outside of tradition and develop my own techniques of sculpting with fibers. I've always been drawn to the softness of fibers and its forgiving nature. This medium has allowed me to explore my fascination with nature through an abstract and vibrant lens.

As an artist dedicated to challenging consumerism and excess, how do you navigate the commercial art world while staying true to your ecological

principles?

As an artist emerging within a digital culture, I've found utilizing commercial art forms such as social media has tremendously helped me grow my profession. I've spent years establishing my Instagram account and as a result, I have a devoted community of fellow artists and collectors who can follow and support my artistic journey. This platform has allowed me to share my ecological principles and bring more awareness to issues such as climate change, the textile waste crisis, and so on.

Your works are often described as inspired by the geometry of biology. Can you elaborate on how the natural world informs the textures, shapes, and colors in your art?

I have a deep fascination with how cells and organisms are formed through patterns and replication. I often use the transformative power of replication of a single form to create my sculptural pieces – building, layering, and structuring my work into something unexpected and quite fascinating.

Source: WOWWART

The magazine cover reads:

BEAUTY PRIME — Celebrating the Visionaries of Beauty

beautyprime.co.uk
ISSUE: 7 - 2026
GLOBAL EDITION

DR. KAVERI KARHADE
Changing The Face Of Dermatology With Science

DR. JURIS BUNKIS
Celebrating Decades Of Expertise In Aesthetic Surgery

The Power Of Simplicity In Skincare
HELEN MORRISON
Leads Frownies Into A New Era Of Innovation And Legacy

Available in

PRINT

Americas to Australia

Europe to Africa Reader's House is available over 190 countries and thousands of retaiers, platforms including Amazon, Barnes & Noble, Walmart, Waterstone's .....

ELECTRONIC

It is an electronic (flip book) format and interactive. Accessable from electronic devices like pc, smart phone, notepads..

ONLINE

All interviews, we conduct make them accessable online for free.

SOCIAL MEDIA

We are on Facebook, Instagram and X. Please follow us on social media @beautyprimemag

contact us today for an interview opportunity at
editor@beautyprime.co.uk

Key Partnerships and Future Initiatives
Expanding the Boundaries of Art and Media

*Being featured in Beauty Prime means gaining visibility
not just in print edition, but across the entire media
spectrum in the US, UK, Europe and beyond*

Key Media Partnerships:

- Associated Press (reaching 50%+ of global population)
- Benzinga (5M monthly visitors)
- Nexstar (68% U.S. TV household penetration)
- Major search engines: Google News, Google, Yahoo, Bing, Ask
- EIN Press Wire coverage
- New Yox Media magazines coverage (Mosaic Digest, Reader's House, CEO Vision, Beauty Prime...)

Broadcast & Digital Coverage:

- Major U.S. network affiliates
- 150+ million monthly radio website users
- 500+ UK media outlets
- Minimum 5 to 20 media placements per country (Albania to Zambia)
- Enhanced SEO positioning with quality backlinks from each media
- Optimized presence on e-commerce platforms)

Distribution Highlights:

- Available through major retailers including Amazon, Barnes & Noble, Walmart, Blackwells and Waterstones
- Available through local retailers Alaska to Wisconsin in the United States.
- Available in print LIFETIME
- Featured across 3000+ media platforms in the US, UK, Europe and beyond

www.ingramcontent.com/pod-product-compliance
Lightning Source LLC
Chambersburg PA
CBHW052347210326
41597CB00037B/6288